LITTLE LEG,

mini saga competition

From The Eastern Counties
Edited by Laura Martin

Disclaimer

Young Writers has maintained every effort
to publish stories that will not cause offence.

Any stories, events or activities relating to individuals
should be read as fictional pieces and not construed
as real-life character portrayal.

 Young**Writers**

First published in Great Britain in 2005 by:
Young Writers, Remus House, Coltsfoot Drive
Peterborough, PE2 9JX
Telephone: 01733 890066
Website: www.youngwriters.co.uk

All Rights Reserved

© Copyright Contributors 2005

SB ISBN 1 84602 318 1

Foreword

Young Writers was established in 1991, with the aim of encouraging the children and young adults of today to think and write creatively. Our latest primary school competition, 'Little Legends', posed an exciting challenge for these young authors: to write, in no more than fifty words, a story encompassing a beginning, a middle and an end. We call this the Mini Saga.

Little Legends From The Eastern Counties is our latest offering from the wealth of young talent that has mastered this incredibly challenging form. With such an abundance of imagination, humour and ability evident in such a wide variety of stories, these young writers cannot fail to enthral and excite with every tale.

Contents

Sam Miller (10)	16
Bobby Portlock (11)	17
Alana Ray (10)	18
Andrew Ray (10)	19
Oak Richardson (10)	20
Cole Stanley (10)	21
James Treadwell (10)	22
Peter Wheatcroft (10)	23

Birchwood Primary School, Martlesham Heath

Marc Goddard (10)	24
Sophie Boggon (10)	25
Chloe Wright (10)	26
Ellie Kett (11)	27
Ryan Youngs (11)	28
Alice Johnson (11)	29
Granby Limb (11)	30
Matthew Harris (11)	31
Debbie Sewell (11)	32
Ross Hare (8)	33

Duncombe School, Hertford

Jessica Hamilton (11)	76
Camilla Beazley (11)	77
Sasha Ewan (9)	78
Isla Couch (11)	79
Jack Howes (10)	80
Jake Courtney (10)	81
Claudia Parrinello (10)	82
Lucy Rose (10)	83
Thomas Anastasiou (10)	84
Lianne Gray (10)	85
Jessica Boyce (9)	86
Karisma Patel (10)	87
Luke Johnston (10)	88
Harrison Banks (10)	89
Charlotte Kiddie (11)	90
Christopher Cheyney (11)	91
Lucie Hayter (10)	92
Holly Armstrong (11)	93
Nick Pomfret (11)	94
Samrita Mudher (11)	95

Katie Crossthwaite (11)	96
Kirsten Lane (10)	97
Francesca Spooner (11)	98
Guy Hewett (10)	99
Charlotte Boyce (11)	100
Victoria Hart (11)	101
Rosanna Trower (11)	102
Aran Shaunak (11)	103
Emma Judkins (11)	104

Giffard Park Combined School, Milton Keynes

Gregory Ross (11)	105
Franziska Dodl (11)	106
Emily Johnson (11)	107
Rebecca Harrington (11)	108
David Penwarne (10)	109
Helen Schmidt (11)	110
Amy Louise Millward (11)	111
Rhys Johnson (11)	112
James Smillie (11)	113

Eloise Charles (11)	114
Matthew O'Connor (11)	115
Ruth Williams (11)	116
Toby Holden (11)	117
Julia Bloomfield (10)	118
Adelle Davidson (10)	119
James Cosby (10)	120

Greyfriars Primary School, King's Lynn

Jack Starling (11)	121
Lindsay Steward (10)	122
Claire Wiggs (11)	123

Grundisburgh Primary School, Grundisburgh

Emily Dow (11)	124
Owen Smith (11)	125
James Jopling (11)	126
Nicky Vince (11)	127
Joe Brown (11)	128
Charlotte Tatham (11)	129

Hall Meadow Primary School, Kettering

Hampton Hargate Primary School, Peterborough

Ethan Barney (8)	144
Ayoub Sebtane (8)	145
Katherine Rowlinson (8)	146
Eden White (8)	147
Rosie Mallows (8)	148
Jordan Lee (8)	149
Chloë Rogers (9)	150
Niamh Kingsley (9)	151
Brittany Askew (8)	152
Nogam El-Sandabesee (9)	153
Kathryn Bailey (8)	154
Zoe Borthwick (9)	155
Josh Edmondson (9)	156
Reece Davis (9)	157

Hartwell CE Primary School, Northampton

Tilly Smith (9)	158
Henry Charter (9)	159

Emma Bruley (9)   160
Charis Evans (9)   161
April Addison (10)   162
Toby Beesley (10)   163
Ryan Martin (10)   164
Jacob Skinner (10)   165
Jamie Skeats (10)   166
Joe Marshall (10)   167
Rhia Shakespeare (10)   168
Jessica Sharp (9)   169
Nicholas Hunter (9)   170
Rhiannon Tidder (9)   171
Jacques Croxford (9)   172

Henham & Ugley Primary School, Bishop's Stortford

Jack Inkley (8)   173
Saffron Parris (8)   174
Stuart Pudwell (8)   175
Charlie Turner (8)   176
Zoe Salmon (8)   177

Francesca Whitelock (8)	178
Charlotte Albiston (10)	179
Sally Reeve-Arnold (10)	180
Adam Machin (10)	181
Eloise Robinson (10)	182
Jessica Hogg (10)	183
Alistair Moore (9)	184
Kathy Foster (8)	185
Eleanor Price (8)	186
George Mortimer (8)	187
Jennifer Graham (9)	188
Chloe Marns (9)	189

Houldsworth Valley Primary School, Newmarket

Shane Parker (9)	190
Tom Houghton (9)	191
Melissa Byrne (9)	192
Sophie Howard (9)	193
Daniel Bristow (9)	194
Jay Preston (9)	195

Aaron Peart (9)   196
Connor Richardson (9)   197
Victoria Murrell (9)   198
Nancy Lane (9)   199
George Gedny (8)   200
Leah Mapston (9)   201
Jena Milne (8)   202

Longthorpe Primary School, Peterborough

Mohd Mitha (10)   203
Emma Chan (10)   204
Katie Jeffries-Harris (9)   205
Megan Gregson (10)   206
Jessica Sharman (10)   207
Bethany Cameron (10)   208
Magda Steele (10)   209
Emily Steele (10)   210
Richard Dodding (10)   211
Daaim Ashraf (11)   212
Hussein-Abbas Ebrahim (9)   213
Ben Johnson (10)   214

Manea Community Primary School, March

Philip Fulcher (11)   254
Sasha Broad (10)   255
Mamiroro Emore (8)   256

St Michael's CE VA Primary School, St Albans

Savanna Guthrie (11)   257
Wynona Dekker (10)   258
Vilma Kallio (10)   259
Jake Branagan (9)   260
Eleanor Morton-Smith (9)   261
Ryan Cobb (9)   262
Emma Pinney (9)   263
Sarah Fabian (9)   264
Emma Ferreira (9)   265
Carys Hogan (10)   266
Joseph Zacaroli (9)   267
William Pettitt (9)   268
Luca Hames (10)   269
Isobel Ryan-Dalton (9)   270
Prasasdini Fernando (10)   271

Summerfield Combined School, Milton Keynes

Charlotte Cooper (10)	289
Sam Hughes (10)	290
James Whitaker (9)	291
Sophie Sankey (10)	292
Kristijan Carlsson (10)	293
Anila Abbas (10)	294
Ryan Watson (10)	295
Damask Talary-Brown (9)	296
April Scott (10)	297
Bilaal Ali (10)	298
Scott Parker (10)	299
Kyle Andrews (10)	300

West Earlham Middle School, Norwich

Alex Howes (12)	301

Wimbotsham & Stow Community School, Kings Lynn

Hayley Clarke (10)	302
Alice Harness (10)	303
Ellen Atkinson (10)	304
Danielle Lamont (11)	305
Corinne Jenkinson (10)	306
Barrie Fletcher (11)	307
Lauren Cox (10)	308
Abbie Silsbury (11)	309
Emma Bates (11)	310
Samuel Warner (11)	311
Jack Hunt (10)	312
Myfanwy-Kate Squires (11)	313
Jedd Desborough (10)	314
Ashley Kidd (11)	315
Brad Wiles (11)	316
Billie McKenzie (10)	317
Jon Corley (11)	318

The Mini Sagas

The Science Of Snot

I don't understand why people are staring – just because an experiment went wrong doesn't make me any different.

As I walk down the street, all eyes on me, I know I should have cleaned my nose. I sneezed, a tidal wave of snot washed them away. *Ha!* That's for staring!

Jack Webb-Heller (11)
Avenue Middle School, Norwich

The Terrible Pizza

The pizza came. Big fat olives, loads of mozzarella.
Mum said, 'It grunted!'
I ate it anyway. On the way home my tummy
heaved.
I heard a voice saying, 'You murdered an olive! Let
me out!'
I don't eat much any longer. I'm too scared. I stick
to peardrops!

Miriam Frank (11)
Avenue Middle School, Norwich

The Blue Aurora

The blue aurora is an illuminated gem found in the heart of a dragon's egg. When touched it gives the nearest being, eternal life and telepathic abilities. The dragon must voluntarily grant possession of the egg, before you lull it to sleep, for the one hour it needs per year.

Stephanie Burt (12)
Avenue Middle School, Norwich

The Haunting

My friends had dared me to go into the haunted house. I approached quietly. I turned the door knob, it creaked open. Inside it was dark. Suddenly there was a loud wailing and white ghostly shadows appeared. I screamed. My friends laughed and took off their bed sheets.

George Bowden (10)
Beachborough School, Brackley

The Scream

Lying on my bed I heard an ear-splitting scream. I
stood up, I clenched my fists. I heard it again, a
cold, blood-curdling yell. It happened every night,
night after night.
When would my sister stop teething?

James Brodey (11)
Beachborough School, Brackley

The Chase

I was running as fast as I could, the boy was chasing me. I hid behind a tree, he saw me. I ran again, he was catching me. I couldn't escape, I ran faster. I turned a corner then I felt a hand on me. 'You're it,' he said.

Aaron Carson (9)
Beachborough School, Brackley

Shooting

I unlocked the cabinet, took out the shotgun and loaded it carefully. I walked out into the sunshine, my legs were trembling. I lifted the gun and aimed it as I'd been shown. *Crack!* It shattered into millions of pieces. I'm getting better at clay pigeon shooting.

Tom Clark (10)
Beachborough School, Brackley

The Sound

I got home after school. No one was there. I ran
into my bedroom shutting the door. Suddenly I
heard something creaking up the stairs. I found a
weapon. A big teddy. That would do. The door
opened, a head peeked in.
'Hello, I'm home!'
Teddy fell on Mum's head.

Oscar Collings (10)
Beachborough School, Brackley

Nerves

Butterflies flutter in my stomach as we walk into
the arena. There is a loud roar. We take our places
in silence, waiting for the signal. A man's arm lifts,
time stands still. *Blast* goes my saxophone, the
concert has begun.

Bethany Deadman (11)
Beachborough School, Brackley

The Missile

He was running straight at me. He lifted his arm
and hurled the missile towards me. Time stood still.
My eyes followed the red blur. It raced through
the air. I held tightly to my bat, I swung it forward
and whacked it hard. The umpire called a six.

Joe Faccenda (10)
Beachborough School, Brackley

Dalek Attack

The ground shook and rumbled as the Dalek moved closer and closer. I leapt out from my hiding place, firing wildly. It turned and aimed straight at me. I ran at it hoping to push it over.

'Wake up Russell, 'Doctor Who' has finished, why are you holding the dustbin?'

Russell Girard (9)
Beachborough School, Brackley

The Drill

Sitting in a chair, a bright light shining in my face. They were questioning me, they made me open my mouth. I could hear a horrible whirring noise, it was coming closer. They were about to put it into my mouth. I closed my eyes. I hate having a filling.

Miranda Green (9)
Beachborough School, Brackley

Silver Figure

I carefully lowered it into the water. Something moved. A silver figure came closer and closer towards me. I froze. It came right by my foot. I gave the line a sharp tug. I pulled it out and held up a fat, glistening trout.

Arisa Kurihara (11)
Beachborough School, Brackley

The Time Bomb

The numbers ticking down, I quickly ran upstairs
My heart pounding, it felt like the end of the
world. The time bomb was about to explode! Then it
started beeping, I knew I was about to die.
My mother said, 'Can you get the cake out of the
oven?'

Henry Lait (10)
Beachborough School, Brackley

The Knight

The tall stone knight raised the glistening axe over his head. Everyone fled in terror, he gave an almighty roar and rushed forward, lashing out in all directions. Body parts flew everywhere. A bell rang, break is over, time to stop reading.

Billy Lawrance-Thorne (10)
Beachborough School, Brackley

The Last Stand

He sat waiting for the call, he started putting on his armour. The battle had begun, he lifted his helmet and lowered it over his head. Now the gloves to grip the weapon, the time had come. He got in position to face the enemy ... He hated being last batsman.

Sam Miller (10)
Beachborough School, Brackley

Falling

I rose into the air, higher and higher. A great force was beneath me. I landed again only to be thrown even further into the sky. My heart gave a leap of fear as I was catapulted upwards. Then I was tumbling and falling. Down, down onto the trampoline.

Bobby Portlock (11)
Beachborough School, Brackley

Cook Out

I looked out of the window, the flames were getting higher. I ran downstairs, I yelled, 'Look, look,' but nobody heard. I raced across the garden, grabbed the tongs and saved the sausages on the barbecue.

Alana Ray (10)
Beachborough School, Brackley

Home Alone

It was dark when I got home from school and read the note, 'Dad and I have gone out, back soon'. Suddenly I heard a noise, the door was opening slowly. I grabbed my cricket bat and lashed out. 'Ow!' said the babysitter.

Andrew Ray (10)
Beachborough School, Brackley

Terror Tuesday

I walked home slowly. It was Terror Tuesday. I lingered as long as I could. Finally I got home. I opened the door slowly and walked into the torture room. Then I picked up last night's dinner plates. I hated loading the dishwasher.

Oak Richardson (10)
Beachborough School, Brackley

The Hunt

I was running down the alleyway looking for the creature, ready to pounce. I could hear it eating something in the dumpster. I put my head in and I saw it. It was brown with black stripes and glowing green eyes.
I said, 'Hi Fluffy, time to go home.'

Cole Stanley (10)
Beachborough School, Brackley

Dad!

I curled up under my covers. I knew he was coming, he always did. Then I heard his big heavy footsteps. They were getting closer and closer. I felt a hand on my foot. It pulled me out from my covers.
'It's time for school,' said Dad.

James Treadwell (10)
Beachborough School, Brackley

Flaming Dragons

I felt danger, the dragons were flaming with anger and started chasing me. They had red scales and golden teeth. I ran into a dead end. I started shaking, my heart was beating hard. Then I froze. Three people appeared out of the dragons and said, 'Happy Chinese New Year.'

Peter Wheatcroft (10)
Beachborough School, Brackley

The Rules Of Physics

He walked towards the tightrope, if the rules of
physics worked he would get to the other building,
if they didn't he would die. They did. He was
walking the tightrope when the building blew up, he
clung onto the building, two firemen helped him up,
he was saved.

Marc Goddard   (10)
Birchwood Primary School, Martlesham Heath

Ferocious Beast

The first steps out of my front door filled me with dread. Heart thumping, hands shaking. Before I knew it I was there. The classroom was in front of me. I touched the handle wondering whether to turn it. It suddenly opened independently. There was my teacher. A ferocious beast!

Sophie Boggon (10)
Birchwood Primary School, Martlesham Heath

The Knock

Knock, knock, knock. Jane swiftly advanced toward the window to look out. *Crack!* The glass shattered. Jane ran and dived under her bed. The door creaked slowly open, *tap ... tap ...* closer ... closer ... she shuddered, her heart thumped quickly and then

...

'Hi Sis, why are you hiding?'

Chloe Wright (10)
Birchwood Primary School, Martlesham Heath

The What?

The What lives in the deep dark woods under the
dirty old bridge. In the night it jumps out and
gobbles everything near it up.
Katie said, 'It's called: Ping-Pong - Jump Along -
The Snail Eater - The Night Creeper.'
But when I told my mum she said,
'The What?'

Ellie Kett (11)
Birchwood Primary School, Martlesham Heath

In The Jungle

In the jungle there was a tiger. It was sleeping so I had to creep past it by pushing my way through the dense jungle plants. Suddenly one of its eyes opened and it blinked. I was shivering with fear.

Ryan Youngs (11)
Birchwood Primary School, Martlesham Heath

Stick Man

There's a piece of paper and a pencil. The pencil is
picked up. It draws a line. Then two legs. Two arms.
A head. Two eyes and a smile.
'Hello,' said the stick man.
The paper's screwed up and thrown in the bin.
'Let's try again,' said the real man.

Alice Johnson (11)
Birchwood Primary School, Martlesham Heath

Help!

I was trapped in the burning building with flames slowly surrounding me. My only escape was the window, which wouldn't open wide enough! Quickly I grabbed the nearest chair and started pounding the window. 'Help! Help!'
Finally the window shattered and I leapt out just as the flames closed in.

Granby Limb (11)
Birchwood Primary School, Martlesham Heath

Meteorite Strike

I was in my spaceship when there was a big jolt. I went to see what it was. It was a meteorite, it had made a huge hole in the spaceship. It went hurtling through space back to Earth and crashed on North America.

Matthew Harris (11)
Birchwood Primary School, Martlesham Heath

The Fiver

One day I went to the football ground. I sat in my favourite stand, waiting. The match started, they scored, they scored another. Then it went black. A shadow came over me. A man behind fell on me! He gave me a fiver. Now I am a happy bunny!

Debbie Sewell (11)
Birchwood Primary School, Martlesham Heath

The Dark Spooky

When I came home my light went out. It was very dark and I couldn't see! I tripped over something and hurt my knee. I felt something touch my shoulder. I felt nervous and scared. I heard footsteps. Suddenly the light came back on! It was only my dad.

Ross Hare (8)
Birchwood Primary School, Martlesham Heath

Untitled

'Oh I do hope this potion works,' said the high witch. The potion was sizzling. She took a spoonful outside. 'Do you want to try this?' she asked a stranger walking by. 'It tastes of apple.'
'OK,' she said. She tried it and dissolved into the ground!

Anisha Gathani (9)
Birchwood Primary School, Martlesham Heath

The Lab

He was there in front of it, it was a huge cave, he entered. It was dark. He found a light, though it was dim. He approached the light, it was a lab. It had wires everywhere. He looked around. He heard a *boom!* The cave caved in.

Ryan Smith (10)
Birchwood Primary School, Martlesham Heath

The Pride

There he lay dozing in the sun with his pride. His cubs playing in the African sunset. The parents were tired after a whole day of hunting ... no food. They needed the food for their cubs, as they were growing thinner each day.
What would happen to the pride ... ?

Hannah Farthing (11)
Birchwood Primary School, Martlesham Heath

The Book

I woke to a start. I could hear a group of chimps in the distance. Suddenly I felt a rumble. I turned round and then I saw a group of elephants thundering towards me ... Then I realised I had to turn the page.

Tristan Finbow (11)
Birchwood Primary School, Martlesham Heath

At The Church

It was at a church where Leo was waiting for his mum to pick him up from Sunday school. He went out to find her. He felt like someone was following him. Suddenly he tripped and a hand grabbed his leg pulling him down!

Vanessa Hewett (11)
Birchwood Primary School, Martlesham Heath

The Haunted House

The house was quiet and appeared haunted. One day, Billy, was walking past the haunted house. Suddenly Billy stopped, he heard a creak. The front door burst open. Out flew a ghost! Behind walked out a mummy. Billy was getting surrounded. Then a vampire bat came out. Billy shouted, *'Help!'*

Daniel Howgego (8)
Birchwood Primary School, Martlesham Heath

The Alien

Once there lived two children.
'I wished we lived with Mum and Dad,' said Owen.
'I don't,' said Olivia. 'We don't go to school.'
'What is the matter Olivia?'
'A green ear,' said Olivia.
'I'll go and have a look,' said Owen.
'Be careful, don't get hurt,' said Olivia.

Kayleigh Garriock (8)
Birchwood Primary School, Martlesham Heath

The Robber That Goes On Holiday

Once there was a town, with a robber. Everyone was scared. Even the king! But the robber was getting old and wanted to retire. He went to Cyprus but the police were there. The police were even in the hotel.

'What am I going to do?' shouted the robber desperately.

Philippa Yates (8)
Birchwood Primary School, Martlesham Heath

The Mysterious Object

Max, the leader of the ranch, was on his way through the canyon. Suddenly he heard a loud *crash! Boom!* In the distance he saw an egg-shaped aeroplane. As he galloped nearer to the object, it suddenly flew off in the distance leaving a cloud of filthy dust behind.

Shubhangi Sharma (8)
Birchwood Primary School, Martlesham Heath

The Crying Alien

Bluey the bird had no friends then something flew,
it was a tear. He got angry as he didn't like crying.
He saw an alien who was also upset. 'Please don't
cry,' said Bluey, 'You can be my friend.'
'OK,' said the alien happily.

Mason Dowden (8)
Birchwood Primary School, Martlesham Heath

A Fast Minute

She climbed in the front seat, her heart pounding
and her body sweating. She got ready to go ...
Suddenly it sped off. She sat there holding on
tight screaming. Then suddenly it stopped. As she
climbed out there was a voice,
'Was the ride good?' asked her mother smiling.

Georgina Lee-Clifton (11)
Birchwood Primary School, Martlesham Heath

Blood Rusted Axe

So cold. King Iron Axe called his dwarf warriors to the old splintered gate.
'Death is near for many of you,' yelled the warmaster angrily clenching his hammer. The gate shook vigorously. 'Here they come, get ready!' The door crashed open! The goblins are here! *Argh!*

Adam Sach (11)
Birchwood Primary School, Martlesham Heath

The Dragon

A thousand years of waiting. Then the sound of marching came to his ears. Finally the dragon people, they were here. He smiled his evil smile and his people started going down the vast mountain. The warriors were waiting but they were no match for the greatest golden dragon king.

Oliver Bennett (10)
Birchwood Primary School, Martlesham Heath

A Damp, Lonely Death

It was a dark, misty night. I came out to find my
father on the farm, I came to call him in. I
followed large footprints. Then suddenly I fell
down the damp old well by the river.
When they found me, it was too late ... I was
already dead.

Siobhan Kelly (11)
Birchwood Primary School, Martlesham Heath

Leap Of Faith

Walking towards the tower, my heart was pounding rapidly. I climbed up the tower not daring to look down. The wind blew by my ears and I heard the cries of a dying wolf. I pulled myself onto the platform some twenty foot high, and I leapt into the air!

Nicola Dijon (11)
Birchwood Primary School, Martlesham Heath

Faith

Two men were in a café. One was Muslim, one was
Hindu, and they started to argue.
'There is no Allah,' one said.
'I disagree, where is Braham now?' the other
questioned.
'Neither of you are right, I am, I'm Christian,' said
a waiter.
And they are still arguing today.

Zachariah Wynne (11)
Birchwood Primary School, Martlesham Heath

Beast Kill

The beastmen were closing in on Ruglud's orcs.
'Fire,' yelled Ruglud.
The orcs released their arrows into the beastmen.
Ruglud's arrow had gone into the neck of a wickedly
horrid chieftain and blood was frothing around the
hole in the neck of the beast.

Craig Nelson (11)
Birchwood Primary School, Martlesham Heath

I Have You Now

The ship was rocking when the captain suddenly shouted, 'The map, it's the map! Someone get it, quick!'
A crew member swam to it and grabbed it, but he disappeared screaming. Then all the other crew members disappeared, screaming.
Then a voice said to the captain, *I have you now!*

Daniel Hodge (11)
Birchwood Primary School, Martlesham Heath

The Mysterious Mist!

Very slowly Milly got out of her crumpled bed,
crept downstairs, flung open the door. Milly ran
down to Ashbrooke Castle, so fast, she flew
through the torn doors of the castle. Suddenly she
tumbled over a jagged nail into some grey tar-like,
mist – nobody has seen her since!

Evie Catt (11)
Birchwood Primary School, Martlesham Heath

The Dream

One day Dan went to space and brought back two
aliens and scared his mum. *'Boo!'*
'Argh!' cried Mum.
'The aliens are taking over the world,' shouted Dan.
'Go and put them back where they came from,' said
Mum.
'No,' I don't want to go,' shouted Dan.

Sophie Fisk (8)
Birchwood Primary School, Martlesham Heath

My Magic Powers

Tesco was very busy one Saturday. Ashley and Max went to Tesco to buy some things for their kind mum. Suddenly, as they got to the meat counter, Ashley's powers began. Max's too. Suddenly the chicken started to fly. Then they told their mum they had very, very special powers.

Emelia Boggon (8)
Birchwood Primary School, Martlesham Heath

The Lost Horse!

It was standing there in its field grazing on the grass when all of a sudden there was a squeaking sound and the gate to the field flung open. The horse galloped out and ran away. The horse stopped and grazed. The owner found the field open. Where was it?

Jessica Hazelton (11)
Birchwood Primary School, Martlesham Heath

The Magic Land

Once there was a magic land that had two fairies
called Tumble and Tinkerbell. One day, Tumble
went out to collect a child's tooth, but he didn't
come back.
'Oh no,' said Tinkerbell. 'What shall I do? They
might catch me too if I go and find him!'

Jade Excell (8)
Birchwood Primary School, Martlesham Heath

Wanted Kidnapper

I was walking to my friend's house when I found myself being shoved into a shed. My ears pricked and I heard thunder. I saw fire, the shed was on fire. Suddenly paramedics were by my side pushing me into an ambulance.

Abigail Turner (10)
Birchwood Primary School, Martlesham Heath

The Lost Car!

His wife went in his new car, he rose and got changed. When he went out into his garage, the car wasn't there. He started to get worried so he phoned the emergency line. Next minute he saw a car the same as his.

'Hello love.'

'Oh thank goodness!'

Elizabeth Catling (10)
Birchwood Primary School, Martlesham Heath

Swimming In Water

It was Sunday and I had a swimming race. The lady said, 'Get ready, on your marks, get set, go.' As I was swimming down the lane I could feel everyone watching me. So I knew I had to win the race. At the end I won the race!

Emma George (10)
Birchwood Primary School, Martlesham Heath

A Close Encounter

There was something flashing in the air. It couldn't be ... it was. A UFO! It landed next to me and out came an alien. So I ran and ran. The alien probe went around the city destroying buildings. The army gathered and shot down the UFO.

Thomas Smith (10)
Birchwood Primary School, Martlesham Heath

A Midnight Gallop

She listened for sound. Then saw the midnight horse! She jumped and galloped in darkness. It reared at a star. She wished this was real, though she knew she'd wake soon. Before knowing it, she was in bed. She woke, and saw the star! It's a dream ... don't you think?

Rosie Steward (10)
Birchwood Primary School, Martlesham Heath

Trotting Tragedy

She was riding, 'Trot on,' speedily the pace
quickened. Suddenly a squirrel dashed out, 'Steady!'
but too late, the horse bucked and she was
catapulted into the air. Time stopped, blackness.
She knew she was injured. Hearing a voice,
'Get up!'
She shot up, she was trotting, she wasn't dreaming.

Rebecca Bowles (10)
Birchwood Primary School, Martlesham Heath

Oops ...

We were exploring the cliff in town. We were having fun until I looked down ... my mum came looking for me. My mum saw me on the cliff, she told me off. We went home and my mum grounded me. I was upset. I didn't know why she grounded me.

Katie Bassingthwaighte (10)
Birchwood Primary School, Martlesham Heath

The Alien Who Landed On The Hill

There was a farmer who lived on a farm. One day an alien spaceship landed on the hill. The farmer thought it was a dog so he took it to the pet shop. In the morning it was on the news. A little girl loved aliens, she wanted one!

Morgan Lankester (8)
Birchwood Primary School, Martlesham Heath

An Alien Visiting Ipswich

There was an alien and an alien dog. They were called very silly names, Q5 and D8. They landed in Ipswich and Q5 shot all the shops and everything in sight.

Everybody was rushing off in their cars, but one man stayed there and said, 'Go back to your planet!'

Daniel Smith (8)

Birchwood Primary School, Martlesham Heath

Coral Reef

One sunny day, Puffer Jackson and Fidget went to
the park. Puffer swam past a little girl. Suddenly,
*pop! E*veryone looked back.
'Oh no, I've popped her balloon.'
Then her mum shouted at Puffer.
An hour later, she found Puffer at the ice cream
van and said,
'I'm really sorry.'

Megan Wright (8)
Birchwood Primary School, Martlesham Heath

The Magic House

The house on the side of town was a magic house.
Knan the dog, Pip, Jack and Jim the owners were
locked out. One day the magic house turned its
roof to mountains. It started singing and going
crazy. They tried to bang and barge the door. They
fell over.

Bailey Reid (8)
Birchwood Primary School, Martlesham Heath

Robot Wreck

Sarah and Cloe were going to a wedding when they decided to skip across the bay. Sarah slipped on some seaweed and fell into the sea. Sarah could not swim, so Cloe came after her, thinking that they would get there, but instead they met Zippy and Zappy, robots.

Hannah Limb (8)
Birchwood Primary School, Martlesham Heath

The Little Bug

I went to the funfair and on the first ride I went
on I met a little bug. It had small ears. It was fat
with shiny legs. I told my mum.
She said, 'What's it called?'
I said, 'The funfair bug.'

Emma Lodge (11)
Birchwood Primary School, Martlesham Heath

The Hairdressers

Once my mum had long hair, until she had a trip to the hairdressers. She wanted just a trim and what she got was a near bald head. Mum got a refund and 40% off her price paid. When we got home my mum put a hat on straightaway.

Tom Hardy (11)
Birchwood Primary School, Martlesham Heath

The Alien Who Invaded The Football Match

Damian and Daniel were playing football in the field with Damian's new Champion's League football. His dad had bought it for him as a present. His dad was very nice to him. Suddenly out of the blue something was in the sky. It was an alien from outer space.

Evan Durance (8)
Birchwood Primary School, Martlesham Heath

An Alien Visits Earth!

An alien was in space looking for the planet Earth,
then suddenly, *crash!* The alien crash-landed on
Earth.
'What on earth was that?'
'Let's go and look outside in the garden.'
'Wow! An alien spaceship. Let's go and have a closer
look!'
'Wow, fabulous equipment, it's brilliant!'

Matthew Hoy (8)
Birchwood Primary School, Martlesham Heath

The Alien Who Visits Earth And Causes Mayhem!

Once there was an alien from outer space, and he went to visit Earth. He was on the wrong planet, he was heading for Mars. He landed in a deserted desert and someone saw him, so he caused mayhem, then he went back to his planet.

Ryan Harvey (8)
Birchwood Primary School, Martlesham Heath

The Dream

I had a dream of me sleeping with a lion and it ate me at midnight. I awoke in a jungle with a lion licking me. The lion and I talked all day, until it was time for bed. I woke up, or did I?

Heidi Cooper (10)
Birchwood Primary School, Martlesham Heath

A Very Hazy Dreamy Happening

I hid silently in the dark night. I saw tiny creatures gathering at a giant mushroom. One spotted me ... They stood me on the mushroom. *Flash!* I was standing on a tree stump gazing at the enchanting surroundings. I fell! All went dark ... down ... down I went, *thud!*

Eloise Vest (10)
Birchwood Primary School, Martlesham Heath

No!

He was sweating all over. His hand was tightly
clenched and nobody could prise it open. He was
running as fast as his little legs could carry him. He
had now ran quite a way and he was tiring. Suddenly
a man grabbed him.
'You can't take it!' he yelled.

Jessica Hamilton (11)
Duncombe School, Hertford

Lost In A Supermarket

'Oh no, I've lost my mum in the supermarket,' she said. 'She was going to get the chicken but she's not in the frozen food section! Shall I go and tell someone? I'm worried and scared. What if I don't find her? In fact, I'm terrified. Oh look there she is!'

Camilla Beazley (11)
Duncombe School, Hertford

Charlotte And The Snake

While Charlotte and her mum were camping, a storm struck! The animals fled, a snake slithered into Charlotte's tent. Mum found her lying with her foot swollen. They rushed to hospital. Nurses at the hospital put her in a bed. She had to stay for a day but she's okay.

Sasha Ewan (9)
Duncombe School, Hertford

Smile

Maddy had been entered as a fashion model in a magazine by her friend, Mandy, for her birthday. One month later, she received a letter from the company. She had got the place. Finally, she was staying in Bristol, smiling away posing for the camera. She couldn't smile before.

Isla Couch (11)
Duncombe School, Hertford

The Scary Storm

Mum shouted, 'Time for bed Jack.'
'But Mum,' said Jack, scared. 'There is a
thunderstorm and I don't like storms.'
But Mum didn't listen. Jack went upstairs scared,
but he remembered what Dad said,
'Never be afraid of anything.'
Jack tried to but he couldn't. Jack screamed,
'Argh.' *Bang!*

Jack Howes (10)
Duncombe School, Hertford

The Sleepover

Why do I have such a massive fear of sleeping at someone's house? I jumped off the bus and walked happily to Bob's house. I went in but he wasn't there. I felt more frightened. Suddenly something pierced through my flesh and all I could feel was excruciating pain.

Jake Courtney (10)
Duncombe School, Hertford

The Secret Garden

Anna lived in a mansion, locked in her bedroom, never allowed out. Every morning she gazed out at the world. Her eyes were drawn to a locked gate. Every day she felt disappointment. One day to her surprise it was open. She could see through. There was the Garden of Eden.

Claudia Parrinello (10)
Duncombe School, Hertford

Death On Ice

One cold, motionless day, a fairy, so pale, sat on a flower. While she was sitting, she noticed a lake underneath; her hand had been frozen. Suddenly a mighty wind blew her off the flower and she fell on the ice. Her death was cold, her blood was blue.

Lucy Rose (10)
Duncombe School, Hertford

Car Crash

In a rush Dad put his foot down. My eyes flicked to the speed dial, 50 … 80. 'Dad,' I screamed, closing my eyes as we reached 125mph. Dad steered round a deer. A car came. *Crash!* My back jolted. Dad was lying on the bonnet. We went off to hospital.

Thomas Anastasiou (10)
Duncombe School, Hertford

Scared

There was a knock on the door. I crept downstairs.
Should I open it or not? I was not sure, 'Yes, I will
open it.' So I did. It was a person with a black
cloak. I looked, I screamed. Oh yeah, it's
Hallowe'en, it's just my friend scaring me.

Lianne Gray (10)
Duncombe School, Hertford

The Sleepover

We laid their awake, scared. He was waking us
silently. We shivered, but said nothing and waited.
He was there and we both knew it! Just then the
door burst open. It was him. We ran and ran but it
was too late, and just like that we were gone.

Jessica Boyce (9)
Duncombe School, Hertford

The Injured Dolphin

I was swimming with leaping, dancing dolphins.
There appeared an amazing sparkly dolphin who
could do flips in the air. I spotted a man strangling
a dolphin, security called the RSPCA. They arrived
and asked us to get out of the water, sorted out
the man. The dolphin was better.

Karisma Patel   (10)
Duncombe School, Hertford

The Disaster

It was dark, darker than the blackout. A bead of sweat trickled down my face. Then something sent shivers down my spine. The ground was shaking. Suddenly a massive explosion sounded like the death of the sun. The fire was coming closer, closer, closer, until …

Luke Johnston (10)
Duncombe School, Hertford

Scared

I'm on board, my seatbelt is fastened. My hands
are sweaty. I can't breathe properly. *'Keep calm!'*
I'm telling myself.
The pilot says, 'Prepare to take off.'
We're now 10,000 feet in the air, that was not too
bad. I will never be scared of flying again.

Harrison Banks (10)
Duncombe School, Hertford

The Football Match

Lola went to the match. She was getting very excited because her team were winning. Later, Lola came home not feeling well. She looked a bit pale and suddenly fainted.

Minutes later she woke up and heard a siren and began to panic! Who called the ambulance to help Lola?

Charlotte Kiddie (11)
Duncombe School, Hertford

The Scary Night

In front of the scared Tommy stood a two-headed demon gobbling up gravestones. Slowly out of a grave rose a half-man, half-skeleton who stood in a defensive stance in front of the demon. The TV turned blank.
Mum said, 'This film is too old for you.'

Christopher Cheyney (11)
Duncombe School, Hertford

Untitled

I'm not ready to go. Just feeling uncontrollably
sick. Why have I even come here? Stay conscious
Andrew. Keep calm.
'Andrew Parker.'
Oh no, they're calling me!
'Andrew Parker, please come to gate forty eight,
thank you.'
Oh how I hate flying.

Lucie Hayter (10)
Duncombe School, Hertford

The Mystery Murderer

'Bye Katie.' I walked down the dark, dingy road. I looked at my watch, already 9.30. The darkness began to spook me, though I knew it was only my own street. I sensed someone following me. I felt cold hands on my neck! I don't remember what happened after that.

Holly Armstrong (11)
Duncombe School, Hertford

A Scary Jump

I'm falling out of control. I was sweaty and hot
even though there was a constant flow of cold air.
I couldn't stop however desperately I tried, I just
couldn't. Suddenly I was jerked upwards, my eyes
nearly popped out. Now I was floating. I felt safe
once again.

Nick Pomfret (11)
Duncombe School, Hertford

New School

I walked in, everyone staring at me. It didn't feel right, I had butterflies. I hoped to make new friends. The teacher said to sit next to Danni, a really gorgeous girl, a geek was sitting behind me with round glasses and goofy teeth. What do they think of me?

Samrita Mudher (11)
Duncombe School, Hertford

Ghost!

It's my first day at my new school. I'm very scared because it's a very large school. My friend says that a ghost lived there, but I don't believe her, or in ghosts!
One day in the classroom the door opened. I screamed and I never went back there again!

Katie Crossthwaite (11)
Duncombe School, Hertford

The Mini Workers

I could feel men with hammers using all their strength to try and break through a white, curved wall. Gradually, men were dying as a burning heat filled the air around them and it wouldn't go away. 'Mum, thanks for the hot water bottle; it's really helping my headache.'

Kirsten Lane (10)
Duncombe School, Hertford

The Monster

There's a big monster in front of me just waiting, waiting for me to get on him and ride him so he can take me away and I may never be seen again. *Argh!* Then it suddenly stopped and I got off. 'Mum can I do that again?'

Francesca Spooner (11)
Duncombe School, Hertford

The Attack Of The Dinosaur

I'm in the jungle. It is getting darker and darker.
Trees swaying, a rustling bush. Something is there,
it is following me. Help! Help! Someone! It will kill
me, argh!
'Turn that off, Jurassic Park is not suitable. You
shouldn't be watching that, so off you go to bed
now!'

Guy Hewett (10)
Duncombe School, Hertford

Roller Coaster

Each step felt like a thousand. My legs like jelly
and hands shaking uncontrollably. Each separate
heartbeat was ringing in my ears. I sat down and
held on tight, closed my eyes, a scream escaped my
mouth. Suddenly I went this way and that way.
Whoosh! It was all over!

Charlotte Boyce (11)
Duncombe School, Hertford

Lost In A City

The huge objects towered over me. Buzzing noises surrounding me. I was shoved this way and that. Roaring monsters fled above me ... The peel of bells was in the air. I didn't know where to go. I was scared. I was lost in a big noisy city!

Victoria Hart (11)
Duncombe School, Hertford

Driving Test

I was driving fast. There were traffic lights just about to turn red. I tried to put my foot on the brake, but it was the accelerator. I was coming closer. As my examiner became more and more anxious, I slammed my foot on the brake just in time!

Rosanna Trower (11)
Duncombe School, Hertford

What's My Line?

I walk on. Powerful stares, shaking, so nervous. I can't move. The stage is sinking. I'm frozen. The curtain opens. I can't remember my lines! My mouth is dry. It's my cue! I can't speak, forgotten my props. Shut door! Wait, that's it! I'm off. Done it and I was great!

Aran Shaunak (11)
Duncombe School, Hertford

Untitled

I look around, I can't see my parents, they should be back. I see a woman looking exactly like my mother. I run up to her. 'Hey Mum, I lost you then.' But it wasn't her, it was a stranger! Then my mum tapped me on the shoulder,
'Hi Emma.'

Emma Judkins (11)
Duncombe School, Hertford

The Shadow

My heart was pounding, my eyes burning. All of a sudden the door swung open, a figure in the shadows silently glided towards me. My feet trembled, they insisted I run. Too late the figure had me.
'Alfie, wake up,' my dad shouted down my ear.

Gregory Ross (11)
Giffard Park Combined School, Milton Keynes

Tiger

With cold sweat forming, the tiger glared at me! I stared at it not daring to move. I could see my reflection in the gleaming eye. Then it roared like a tremendous storm.

'Peter, don't look out of the window in my maths lesson.'

Franziska Dodl (11)
Giffard Park Combined School, Milton Keynes

Beneath The Water

Its scaly body was swimming round and round, not taking its eyes off me. There was only a thin layer of glass between us. It could jump any moment. It kept coming up for air, never looking away.
Then I heard Mum shouting, 'Tom, have you fed that fish yet?'

Emily Johnson (11)
Giffard Park Combined School, Milton Keynes

The Wand

My heart pounded. It was going to devour me, for sure this time. There was nowhere to run unless ... Unless I used my wand, but it didn't, it couldn't work. I was dead. A gonner. Oh no! Argh ...
'Cut, cut, cut, that's a wrap. Well done boys.'

Rebecca Harrington (11)
Giffard Park Combined School, Milton Keynes

Rain

I was striding home from school when suddenly
miniature bombs started to fall. People were
running for their lives here and there. *'Argh!'* I
screamed and started to run as fast as I could.
My friend Jack, who was scurrying with me, yelled,
'Wait it's rain.'

David Penwarne (10)
Giffard Park Combined School, Milton Keynes

The Surprise

I could feel the rattle of the uncontrolled vehicle.
If it was going to this virtually deserted place, it
must be. Round the corner was doom. The house
came into view as we rounded the bend. A bang
startled me.
'Balloons popped,' Mum said, 'and there's Grandma,
the party girl.'

Helen Schmidt (11)
Giffard Park Combined School, Milton Keynes

The Monster

It was silent, so very silent. There was a creak ... I lay underneath my covers ... I peered out. Nothing was there. I hid underneath my covers gasping for air. 'Uh ... ! What was that?' Shock ran throughout my body! 'Oh no!'
'I want my breakfast *now!*' screamed my little brother.

Amy Louise Millward (11)
Giffard Park Combined School, Milton Keynes

The Alien

It went dark, but there was a glow behind the door. The floorboards creaked, then I heard it - a turning of my bedroom door handle. The alien is coming! Then aaarrrhhh, what is it? No, no! It was my dad! 'Stop tickling me! You know I can't stop laughing.'

Rhys Johnson (11)
Giffard Park Combined School, Milton Keynes

The Thing

There I was, my gun in my hand, my stomach writhing. Suddenly I heard a creak. I could hear breathing. I turned and bolted far away from it as possible, but it was hot on my heels. I let off my gun. Too late. It got me.
Game over boomed the television. *Aww!*

James Smillie (11)
Giffard Park Combined School, Milton Keynes

Argh Monster

I was on the balcony trembling. I was alone.
Suddenly I turned around. Argh! A big hairy
monster was blocking the way. Water filled my
eyes. A light went on, then I fell to the ground
crying. My mum opened the door,
'It's only a spider,' she said, half asleep.

Eloise Charles (11)
Giffard Park Combined School, Milton Keynes

The Dragon

I can hear something coming, a horrifying sound. I saw it, a massive dark green dragon, terrorising me, his jet-black back. He shot red fire out of his mouth, red as the sun. I just realised I had eaten a hot chilli.

Matthew O'Connor (11)
Giffard Park Combined School, Milton Keynes

House Horror

I was alone in the house. Everywhere was deserted.
It was thundering and the sky was inky black.
Someone rang the doorbell. I cautiously opened the
door. A dark, shadowy figure loomed over me. I
screamed shrilly but couldn't move.
'Do you want one bottle or two?' asked the milkman.

Ruth Williams (11)
Giffard Park Combined School, Milton Keynes

Shadow's Story

I remember falling down towards Earth. The last of my chaos energy drained out of my body, like water trickling from a tap. I turned back again to my normal form. I had no power, I was too weak to do anything. I was a plain black hedgehog again, helpless.

Toby Holden (11)
Giffard Park Combined School, Milton Keynes

I've Done A Runner, Get Me Out Of Here!

Running along a small, dank passage. I'm away! I double somersault on a rope. I fall gracefully to the floor. I'm lost. Then, I see a shadow across the ground. I'm enclosed in a round chamber. The last words I hear are,
'What was that spider doing in the classroom?'

Julia Bloomfield (10)
Giffard Park Combined School, Milton Keynes

The Thing

Every time I walked past it I got a cold shiver down my spine. So when I got home from school, I decided to take a look. Slowly I opened the door and then ... *crash!* Scratching and running. I'm never playing hide-and-seek with Luke again.

Adelle Davidson (10)
Giffard Park Combined School, Milton Keynes

War Of The Universe

Lightning struck again and again. Then all was silent. Suddenly a huge metal Titan rose out of the concrete covered ground. Everybody froze in fear. Then the mighty machine declared,
'People of Earth ... Earth ... ? I told you Xacribe we should have turned left at Jupiter ... Sorry Earth people.'

James Cosby (10)
Giffard Park Combined School, Milton Keynes

Humpty Dumpty

He sat on the wall, thinking, picking at the bricks.
He picked the bricks so much the wall collapsed and
he fell off the wall. As he crashed to the ground
his shell was demolished. All the king's men couldn't
put Humpty together again.

Jack Starling (11)
Greyfriars Primary School, King's Lynn

Humpty

Humpty sat on the wall. He started to wobble.
Suddenly he began to lose his balance and was
slipping. Humpty ... fell off the wall and split into
tiny pieces. So all the king's horses and all the
king's men, had scrambled eggs for breakfast again.

Lindsay Steward (10)
Greyfriars Primary School, King's Lynn

Five Alive

Five fruits of the world lay dead at daybreak. They knew night was the time for fun. Night crept closer every minute. Then it arrived. The soulful fruits danced all night long, until at last morning came. Now there's only four alive. What ... ? Why ... ? Where ... ? and how?

Claire Wiggs (11)
Greyfriars Primary School, King's Lynn

The Titanic

The boat had struck the iceberg and now a hole
was made. Everybody fled for life upstairs but
slowly the boat sank. Lifeboats stuffed with women
and children. People jumping overboard, hanging
onto doors and wood in the freezing icy water. Only
some will survive the deadly night.

Emily Dow (11)
Grundisburgh Primary School, Grundisburgh

7th Of July

One day, a normal day, traffic as normal, life as
normal ten seconds before, no one knew anything.
The bombs exploded, life stood still and stopped,
everything in slow motion. The wreckage, the
debris, the dead, the wounded. Terror, this is not
life but death.

Owen Smith (11)
Grundisburgh Primary School, Grundisburgh

The Streets Of America

They walked down the roads scared of nothing, the only thing that got in their way were the birds. People ran inside to take cover. All the shops closed. Silence. All that could be heard was the shrill cry of a baby. The gangsters had taken over the whole world!

James Jopling (11)
Grundisburgh Primary School, Grundisburgh

Thief!

It was a normal day. I walked to school to find police searching everywhere, looking for a stolen laptop. I decided to help. We looked until I spotted a man in the distance with a small package. We caught him, he was put in jail and I got a reward!

Nicky Vince (11)
Grundisburgh Primary School, Grundisburgh

The End

The battle lasted for weeks until finally the victors were the chaos. The dwarves fled with the elves but the Britannians fought and died. The orcs chased them with the dark elves. The elves and dwarves will shelter in the mountains for years until they meet again in Castle Erengrad.

Joe Brown (11)
Grundisburgh Primary School, Grundisburgh

The Curse

She lay still for she had a curse on her. She walked
to the door, a pain ripped at her heart! She
screamed, someone heard. They ran to her but
were too late. She lay still on the floor, her eyes
were grey. She was cold: icy cold ...

Charlotte Tatham   (11)
Grundisburgh Primary School, Grundisburgh

The Smuggler

On the edge of the town there was a deserted beach. In the middle of the beach there was a small, dark wood. Up a tree in the wood there was a wooden tree house. In the tree house there was a smuggler waiting ... watching ...

Emily Grimwood (11)
Grundisburgh Primary School, Grundisburgh

The Spy

'Mission Spy I'll destroy you, the rebellion will
defeat you.'
'Never! I've planted a bomb.'
'The one by the car park?'
'Dang, how do you know?'
'You told me when I was your general, argh! I'm
burning.'
Bing!
'Tom have you been melting toy soldiers in the
microwave again?'

Jack Cutmore (10)
Grundisburgh Primary School, Grundisburgh

Murder In The Fields

One morning the two horses wanted to play a game.
So they got Piggy on the other field to play
football with them. Piggy missed a goal and went
off in a stress, the two horses got bored and went
back to eating, after they'd killed Piggy at half-
time!

Natasha Powney (11)
Grundisburgh Primary School, Grundisburgh

No More Children

The witch was stirring her cauldron for the children she'd locked in her shed. She came outside and shoved the purple liquid down their throats. They disappeared. Her potion had worked. Once two children had tried the potion and disappeared, all the children in the world would vanish.

Alicia Marsh (11)
Grundisburgh Primary School, Grundisburgh

The Worm

One night a man was testing on a worm in his laboratory. He fed it nuclear waste, then suddenly it grew. It grew a mouthful of teeth, horns and devilish red eyes, then it attacked. It rose into the air then leapt. The man jumped into the waste and disappeared.

Finn Bentley (11)
Grundisburgh Primary School, Grundisburgh

Murder

The evil genius was dressed in white. David was laying nearby. He loaded his gun.

'I'm Matthew Goggle-Mouth,' said the genius. David shot the bullet, hit Matthew Goggle-Mouth in the back of the head. He was dead. David felt a jab in the ribs. The man kicked David.

Game over.

James Farthing (11)
Grundisburgh Primary School, Grundisburgh

The Monster!

What I am describing is not human at all. This monstrosity is a monster. He sits lugubriously on his crunched up chair, staring with those piercing red eyes and then, all of a sudden he pounces like a wild cheetah! He's not an animal or a goblin, he's my cousin!

Nathan Barnes (10)
Hall Meadow Primary School, Kettering

The Fall

I tripped, I fell, what was happening? All was black.
I opened my eyes; people rushed around the room.
A man in a white jacket hovered over me. The light
was bright, too bright for my eyes. I suddenly
noticed the blood pouring down my arm.
'Cut!' screeched the director.

Rebecca Goringe (10)
Hall Meadow Primary School, Kettering

Love!

The man lay diseased on the exquisite marble floor. He lay wounded, unwanted. He was dying in enormous pain. His last word was love. This is what the poor man needed to fulfil his need of life. Slowly and slowly God left him. Slowly and slowly he perished ...

Danyal Rahemtulla (11)
Hall Meadow Primary School, Kettering

The Ugly Monster

My door is slowly opening, as it's walking through my room. It's taking my toys and chucking them about, wrecking my room. I cried to my mum and dad, 'Help! Help!' But nobody replied. It is taking four more steps in front of me.
Wait, it's my mum!

Lucy Budworth   (10)
Hall Meadow Primary School, Kettering

Scream!

A car was driving through a desert. A song could be heard. Red dust surrounded the car and the song stopped. Everything was silent except for a scream. The scream was louder than ever. The red was thinning and there stood Geri Halliwell, 'Scream if you want to go faster.'

Huw Skiplorne (10) & Lewis Robinson (11)
Hall Meadow Primary School, Kettering

Goal!

I was just standing there waiting. It was coming closer at incredible speed. Was it going to hit me or miss me? I felt its leathery skin brush past me as it just missed me and smacked at the back of the tattered net. Goal!

Amanda Whitehead (11)
Hall Meadow Primary School, Kettering

Untitled

I live in a cold attic where no one wants me, except for the innocent animals that surround me. I keep warm by sitting next to the fierce fire. I dream of being royal instead of being Cinderella.

Marybeth Douglas (11)
Hall Meadow Primary School, Kettering

Ghost!

It was cold, gloomy. The thunder roared with the rapid wind as the rain shot down from the deathful sky. The street lights were dim, the lightning flashed as the thunder banged. Down shot the thunder onto the road.
'Hhhaaa!' screamed through the mist.
Something evil had come.

Jason Barnes (11)
Hall Meadow Primary School, Kettering

Explosive Chemicals

I was getting really excited because I was going home.
Miss said, 'Home time.'
Everyone rushed into the cloakroom. I ran as fast as I could home to my exciting experiment. *Boom!* The house had exploded, I knew I should have put the experiment much higher. I'm in big trouble.

Ethan Barney (8)
Hampton Hargate Primary School, Peterborough

Dinosaurs Appear

It all happened when the dinosaur appeared in the fog. Lots of them appeared. We pulled back. The T-rexes came towards me, then the triceratops came, then all the others. It got worse and worse. I was really scared, so was my sister, Lucy, even Mum and Dad were scared.

Ayoub Sebtane (8)
Hampton Hargate Primary School, Peterborough

The Gargoyle

It was a full moon! An unusual noise woke up a boy, the boy thought he was dreaming. When he looked outside there was a gargoyle on his window. He let him in, they were both very happy when they could both talk, because they both needed a friend.

Katherine Rowlinson (8)
Hampton Hargate Primary School, Peterborough

The Spell That Went Wrong

Kaboom! Bang! There was smoke covering all of the room, and all the air. We were all coughing. When we looked around there were frogs everywhere jumping on things and knocking things, and potions were over the floor. Making the frogs turn into snakes, tadpoles, then back to themselves.

Eden White (8)
Hampton Hargate Primary School, Peterborough

The Little Goat

Once upon a time there was a goat. He wanted to cross a bridge but he couldn't, so he crossed a river instead. However he didn't know that it was a crocodile-infested river. When the little goat was swimming in the river, the crocodile jumped up and ate him.

Rosie Mallows (8)
Hampton Hargate Primary School, Peterborough

Untitled

Once many years ago there was a violent war. The Vikings were busy defending Jorvik, when a great storm blew up the mighty warrior Hiro high up into the sky. Struggling to get away, lightning hit him. He was killed, but he was reborn as the mighty god, Thor.

Jordan Lee (8)
Hampton Hargate Primary School, Peterborough

The Alien

On a dark, rainy day, Emma came home from school and found out that the back door was open. In she crept. *Creak!* She jumped! She looked down at her red school blazer when a green arm caught her eye. On flicked the light and there she saw, her brother!

Chloë Rogers (9)
Hampton Hargate Primary School, Peterborough

A Pot Of Gold

The leprechaun lay back and relaxed. He looked at his shiny pot of gold. Then he heard a noise. The noise of a beast! He looked. Purple fluff! He got up and saw a phoenix, it cowed and burst into flames. It had used his pot to die peacefully.

Niamh Kingsley (9)
Hampton Hargate Primary School, Peterborough

The Pot Of Gold

One day the leprechaun woke up, while he was guarding his gold. He saw a griffin try to take his gold. So Mr Leprechaun scratched the griffin and the griffin scratched Mr Leprechaun back. Mr Griffin said he only wanted food and didn't mean any harm. They became best friends.

Brittany Askew (8)
Hampton Hargate Primary School, Peterborough

The Dreadful Spell

I broke up with my friend. I wanted to turn her into a frog. 'Froggy, doggy doo, I hate you. You are a frog!' I was expecting her to turn into a frog but my wand was the wrong way round, so I turned into a frog. *Ribbit, ribbit, ribbit.*

Nogam El-Sandabesee (9)
Hampton Hargate Primary School, Peterborough

Tragedy In The Woods

One day Snow White was walking in the woods when an evil knight stabbed her in the heart. She lay there for several days and nobody noticed, then her husband, Prince Peter, started a search party to see if they could find her. She was dead when they found her.

Kathryn Bailey (8)
Hampton Hargate Primary School, Peterborough

Holly's Surprise

It was Holly's birthday in two weeks' time and she hadn't thought about what she wanted. She said to everyone she loved Scoobies, but that was all. Two weeks' later when she came home from school, walked past the lounge door, it opened and her mum jumped out saying,
'Surprise!'

Zoe Borthwick (9)
Hampton Hargate Primary School, Peterborough

The Great Football Match

I was on the way to a football match, Magic United v Ragers Rogers. I got there in time for the match. I was on the front row of the east stand and I was behind the manager, and I got his autograph. I cheered for Magic United Football Club.

Josh Edmondson (9)
Hampton Hargate Primary School, Peterborough

The Moving Staircase

I arrived at my mum's house. I'm afraid of heights. My mum has a really high house, so I started to go up the stairs. It started to move and I felt like I was going to be sick. When I got to the top, it had not even moved!

Reece Davis (9)
Hampton Hargate Primary School, Peterborough

The Party Surprise

Sophie was eleven years old and she was having a party at the community centre. She said, 'Where is everyone? It is four o'clock.'

The room was empty. There wasn't a sound. Suddenly everyone arrived. They all shouted, 'Surprise, surprise' and they had a bright, booming, colourful party.

Tilly Smith (9)
Hartwell CE Primary School, Northampton

Bill's Surprise Party

The clock struck 8pm as Bill returned home. He clambered up the stairs and got changed. Then he grabbed his football and went to the park. On the way he met Ben.
'Come with me,' said Ben.
They went home.
'Surprise!'
What a great party!

Henry Charter (9)
Hartwell CE Primary School, Northampton

Heights!

Tom was scared of heights. His friends wanted to go on a super roller coaster ride. Tom was forced to go on the ride. When he was on the roller coaster he was scared. *'Help!'*
They had a party about being brave and overcoming heights. Tom isn't scared any more.

Emma Bruley (9)
Hartwell CE Primary School, Northampton

A Frog Forever

One sunny day Tom was walking home from school.
He walked through the forest. Suddenly, he met a
wizard. The wizard did a magic spell. It went all
wrong, he turned him into a hideous frog. He could
not turn him back. Tom was a frog for evermore!

Charis Evans (9)
Hartwell CE Primary School, Northampton

Rainbow The Pony

One day when Rainbow the pony came into the field
she found some delicious grass around the pond.
Rainbow jumped the fence to the grass and started
eating it.
The next morning a strange thing happened.
Overnight the grass had grown taller than Rainbow
and stopped.

April Addison (10)
Hartwell CE Primary School, Northampton

The Third World

The last day of the world was coming. Nobody knew when it was coming and then it hit. Everybody ran, panicking, towards the public library. It happened so fast, the end was near. There were buildings frosted all over. It wasn't cold, it was a thousand times worse than that.

Toby Beesley (10)
Hartwell CE Primary School, Northampton

What A Mystery

Francis hung his coat on his coat hanger. He went back downstairs to find his coat had gone. He sprinted outside, the sun going down. He stole everyone's coats which were similar to his. Then he found his wife in the laundry room, washing his coat.

Ryan Martin (10)
Hartwell CE Primary School, Northampton

The Awful Thunderstorm

One night there was an awful thunderstorm. People were terrified. It woke everyone, but in someone's house their front door opened. The people in the house were horrified. Then the floorboards started to creak, someone was walking up the stairs into the room! The electrician was checking the power.

Jacob Skinner (10)
Hartwell CE Primary School, Northampton

The Day We Won The FA Cup

On Saturday we played against a team who we had never heard of before. Our team Bramble United kicked off. By half-time the other team were three-nil up. Bramble United scored four goals in the last ten minutes. The whistle went and we were awarded the FA Cup.

Jamie Skeats (10)
Hartwell CE Primary School, Northampton

The Dark Alley

I was panicking. The alley seemed to grow. My friend was supposed to meet me here an hour ago. I was running through the alley when I tripped. I was recovering when I saw a spooky figure! As the figure was drawing closer I saw it was my friend.

Joe Marshall (10)
Hartwell CE Primary School, Northampton

James Goes For A Goal

On the football pitch James was the only one that
hadn't scored, but usually he always scored. Sam
had scored four and Joe had scored three. But
suddenly he tripped over and smacked his face. The
fans cheered him on, he still carried on and scored,
they won the cup.

Rhia Shakespeare (10)
Hartwell CE Primary School, Northampton

Welcome Home

The house was light and deserted. Beth came home from university. She walked into the sitting room and put down her baggage. Suddenly she heard some giggling from a door surrounding her. It made her suspicious. Then all of a sudden her family let off streamers. They shouted, 'Welcome home!'

Jessica Sharp (9)
Hartwell CE Primary School, Northampton

Trip To A Mansion

Tom was playing football in his garden. A storm came, rain dripped on his face. A portal appeared. Tom jumped in the portal. He was in a mansion. Nine ghosts were marching towards him. Another portal appeared. He dived into the portal, he was back home.

Nicholas Hunter (9)
Hartwell CE Primary School, Northampton

The Alien's Best Birthday Present

After school, the young thin alien came to his ship (which was silent). Where is everyone? He thought he felt like a massive block of ice was down his back. *Beep!* The alien ran like lightning to the nearest door. Slowly, the door opened. *Zap!* Wow! What a ray gun!

Rhiannon Tidder (9)
Hartwell CE Primary School, Northampton

Alley Of The Zombies

The new house was boring so I went for a walk and went into a deserted alleyway. I was running and I tripped on a green, slimy stone. When I was on the cold, wet floor I heard some heavy footsteps. A zombie bit me. I never came home.

Jacques Croxford (9)
Hartwell CE Primary School, Northampton

Doctor Who

'Where are we?' said Rosey.
'Planet Zog,' Doctor replied. He opened the door
Rraahh! He slammed it shut.
'What was that Doctor?'
'Alien,' he replied. 'We need to destroy it. I need to
test its blood. I need to make a gun.' He did. He
opened the door and fired.

Jack Inkley (8)
Henham & Ugley Primary School, Bishop's Stortford

Haunted Or Not Haunted

Sam went in the house and heard dripping, he
investigated. It wasn't water, it was blood! He
heard scratching and a voice –
'We'll do it today!'
He rushed and got his mum. She said the blood was
just water, the scratching was a dog and the voices
were removal men.

Saffron Parris (8)
Henham & Ugley Primary School, Bishop's Stortford

Fishing In Loch Ness

I fish in Loch Ness for hours. I wait, then suddenly a bite! Rod bends wildly then jump, the monster of the Loch! I reel slowly, carefully, tail slapping the water. Closer, razor-sharp teeth, slimy and green urging forward. Almost at shore, line breaks under strain! Monster gone.

Stuart Pudwell   (8)

Henham & Ugley Primary School, Bishop's Stortford

Galaxy Adventures

There was Falin. I drew out my light sabre when he did. I leapt over him and stabbed him. I ran into a chamber. There in front of me were droids. Behind them was the diamond! I swung my light sabre round and got the droids. Then I got the diamond. *'Whoopee!'*

Charlie Turner (8)
Henham & Ugley Primary School, Bishop's Stortford

Suzi And The Creepy Castle

Suzi's hands trembled as she opened the door to the castle. Was it there? The ghost of the chamber of secrets. She pushed the door widely and stepped in. Something was in there. That something took the picture off the wall and let it crash to the ground.
'Argh!'

Zoe Salmon (8)
Henham & Ugley Primary School, Bishop's Stortford

Going Into Space

Going into space, the rocky surface under my feet.
I take a step, I bounce up in the air. I think I will
never come back. The sun shines brightly. No plants
grow here, no rivers flow but I see some
footprints. I go back to the rocket.

Francesca Whitelock (8)
Henham & Ugley Primary School, Bishop's Stortford

Scared And Still!

I wake up at night. I stay sitting as I hear the
fireworks go off, *bang! Bang!* Frozen, suddenly it
stops, silence at last. Then again, *bang! Bang!*
Scared and still. Colourful patterns in the sky, but
I'm still scared. The door creaks open, what is it?
It's *Mum!*

Charlotte Albiston (10)
Henham & Ugley Primary School, Bishop's Stortford

Force

'*Who's there? Who's talking?*' Thoughts spun through Joe's head as he frantically looked around, his heart was pounding in his chest. He looked into the lake in time to see a hand reaching out to him. Joe's breathing became intense as he ran. He realised he'd been imagining things.

Sally Reeve-Arnold (10)
Henham & Ugley Primary School, Bishop's Stortford

The Spy

They locked me in a room. I heard an explosion,
there I was in a burning building. I knocked the
door down, I saw smoke. I ran to the bottom floor.
There were flames and the floor was burning. I
ran. The floor broke, I jumped and landed safely.
Phew!

Adam Machin (10)
Henham & Ugley Primary School, Bishop's Stortford

Surprise!

Lucy was worried. Her cat Icicle was looking ill and getting fat. But she wasn't eating. One day Icicle was nowhere to be seen. Lucy asked her mum but she didn't know. Lucy went to her room. There, under her bed was Icicle and three cute kittens.

Eloise Robinson (10)
Henham & Ugley Primary School, Bishop's Stortford

Help!

Up the stairs and through the door I see a man. He
sees me looking at him, as he says,
'Don't say a word.'
'You have our stuff,' I say.
He races down the stairs. I chase after him. 'Help,
he is taking our stuff!' Oh, it was the removal man.

Jessica Hogg (10)
Henham & Ugley Primary School, Bishop's Stortford

The Big Bang

I was playing on my PS2 and I heard a bang! What was that? I went out to the backyard. I saw a spaceship, I saw an ugly alien. It had green skin, red goggle eyes, a very big head and short arms. Suddenly *whoosh* and they were gone!

Alistair Moore (9)
Henham & Ugley Primary School, Bishop's Stortford

The Fairies In A Magnificent World

'Hello,' said a kind voice. 'Are you OK?' It was a fairy! It ran away. So I followed it to a toadstool. There I saw magnificent fairies. I heard a strange noise. I woke up. It must have been a dream. But there was a twinkle behind the curtains? Fairies!

Kathy Foster (8)
Henham & Ugley Primary School, Bishop's Stortford

The Wild Experiment

One day I was daydreaming in the classroom. I was
doing an experiment. I put in vinegar and sugar,
pepper and salt ... Oops! I wasn't meant to put in
salt ... ! *Bang!*
'Eleanor, clear up that mess.'
'But ...'
'No buts!'
'I was just trying to make a little dog.'
'Go now!'

Eleanor Price   (8)
Henham & Ugley Primary School, Bishop's Stortford

The Birdians

They came in July on a dark night. I heard a splat.
I woke the next morning, a crop circle had
appeared in a field. It was the shape of a bird.
Then a laser shot through the roof. I was abducted
by the Birdians. I woke on the ground.

George Mortimer (8)
Henham & Ugley Primary School, Bishop's Stortford

The Alien Who Travelled To Earth

There was an alien who landed on Earth. Everyone in the town was afraid of him, so he made a house in a ditch so people couldn't see him. He saw a man drop a bottle of petrol. He picked it up and poured it in his ship and disappeared.

Jennifer Graham (9)
Henham & Ugley Primary School, Bishop's Stortford

The Experiment

Potions bubbling any colour you can think of. People
turning into things, robots, monsters. My brain is
exploding with ideas. My heart is thumping harder
and harder, *thump, thump*. Mixing potions pink and
purple, green and blue.
'Jane are you listening to my medical lesson?'

Chloe Marns (9)

Henham & Ugley Primary School, Bishop's Stortford

Worm's Life

I was hiding under the earth. I could see something pecking on the earth. The others ran away, but I stood there wondering what was going on. A yellow beak picked me up. I screamed silently, it was the early bird. I was the worm.

Shane Parker (9)
Houldsworth Valley Primary School, Newmarket

It's A Rabbit's Life!

I was playing with my brother. I heard a wolf. I was scared. My brother ran out the burrow screaming. Five seconds later I did the same. I was eaten. The wolf had two rabbits that night and happily went to sleep.

Tom Houghton (9)
Houldsworth Valley Primary School, Newmarket

The Little Pig

The little pig was in his house and he saw a wolf,
then looked out the other window and saw another
wolf. He looked out the door and crept behind a
tree and looked at his house. The wolf was not
there.

Melissa Byrne (9)
Houldsworth Valley Primary School, Newmarket

Devil Castle

I entered Devil Castle. I crept into the darkness a little more. I ran right up the stairs and I looked around. There was a pair of binoculars. I picked them up and looked through them – there was a monster! I looked on the lens – only a caterpillar.

Sophie Howard (9)
Houldsworth Valley Primary School, Newmarket

Under The Sea

I'm under the sea, a monster is killing everyone. I'm running out of oxygen and I'll be lucky to survive. Oh no! I can see something moving, the ground is shaking. What is it? What is it? It's the Loch Ness monster. I must be dead.

Daniel Bristow (9)
Houldsworth Valley Primary School, Newmarket

The Beauty And The Beast

There stood Beauty at the bottom of the stairs, afraid of the beast. Footsteps stomping down the staircase. She peered round the corner and started to catch a glimpse of the beast's bed. Oh no! It's the beast's chamber pot!

Jay Preston (9)
Houldsworth Valley Primary School, Newmarket

The Hunt For Gold

I had been looking for gold for many days. When a storm broke out and a huge wave knocked me overboard. I was swallowed whole by a scaly sea monster.
When I awoke in its stomach I was surrounded by all the gold I wanted, but was trapped forever!

Aaron Peart   (9)
Houldsworth Valley Primary School, Newmarket

Little Red Riding Hood

Little Red Riding Hood was quivering behind a tree. She was looking for Wolf, but she couldn't see Wolf. 'Where did he go?' she asked. Suddenly the wolf jumped out behind her and how Miss Hood ran for her life and the wolf followed her, then ate her up.

Connor Richardson (9)
Houldsworth Valley Primary School, Newmarket

The Slow Snail

The slow snail was slithering out of his unstable house when he heard a bird coming to get him. He slithered away, but he was too slow. The bird got the snail and started chewing. Then he spat it out. It was disgusting. Birds don't like snails.

Victoria Murrell (9)
Houldsworth Valley Primary School, Newmarket

The Sad Cheetah

The sad cheetah lay in the hot desert grass waiting
for something exciting to happen. Just then a
penguin came along,
'Hello there chap, I'm having a race tonight –
coming?'
The cheetah smiled. The race started. As the
cheetah was running he tumbled, the sad cheetah
came in last.

Nancy Lane (9)
Houldsworth Valley Primary School, Newmarket

The Postman

My family has a postman. He is very jolly and funny.
One day he came to deliver our mail. It was
someone else! He was not so jolly and not funny. He
delivered our mail for weeks, but the truth was he
was really wearing a mask! It was him!

George Gedny (8)
Houldsworth Valley Primary School, Newmarket

The Ghostly Horse

It was a ride like no other. I was trotting in the woods when suddenly my horse spooked and jerked into a gallop. I was afraid. I looked back and saw it – the ghostly horse, shimmering in the moonlight. It jumped straight through me. I never rode again!

Leah Mapston (9)
Houldsworth Valley Primary School, Newmarket

The Naughty Pig

The naughty pig was sneaking around to see if there was anything that he could destroy. He went around the most extraordinary houses and he couldn't find anything to destroy. He found a huge spider, the naughty pig was scared. He saw the spider again. It was a toy spider.

Jena Milne (8)
Houldsworth Valley Primary School, Newmarket

The Mystery

One day I was on my way home from a friend's house. I saw someone weird and I chased him. He disappeared. So I carried on. When I reached home I went in there. I heard something break really loud. Everyone shouted, '*Boo!*'

Mohd Mitha (10)
Longthorpe Primary School, Peterborough

Tent Terror

Whoosh! Our tent felt like it had gone round like a washing machine. Suddenly a light beamed into our tent! We scrambled under the sleeping bags. As the thing got closer we grabbed our pillows and threw them at the thing. The thing was a very, very, very mad mum.

Emma Chan (10)
Longthorpe Primary School, Peterborough

The Thing

Hannah screamed, the thing was coming closer. She tried running away. There was no escape. She looked for the light switch but couldn't find it. She screamed again. The door opened and the light switched on. The thing was there, in front of her! It was Dad with his tools!

Katie Jeffries-Harris (9)
Longthorpe Primary School, Peterborough

Untitled

'Washing machines live longer with Calgon!' beamed the handsome advert presenter. At that moment the washing machine rumbled.

'Roar!' ranted the washing machine as it grew into the terrifying wash monster.

'Argh!' screamed the people, 'Quickly!'

The Calgon was put into the washing machine to save the people.

Megan Gregson (10)
Longthorpe Primary School, Peterborough

We Come In Peace

News headlines, 'Aliens land on Earth. Will they attack? Or will they come in peace? Today in town square five aliens came to scavenge the land to find their master who was captured 5000 years ago. We have to get them off this planet before they destroy everyone.'

Jessica Sharman (10)
Longthorpe Primary School, Peterborough

Dreading Bed!

The sky became dark, wind absailed down the building. 'It's night all right!' I said as I forced my eyes open and hid under the sheets. The troll entered, demanding for me to go to sleep. But then lightning hit the building as the figure fell to the floor.

Bethany Cameron   (10)
Longthorpe Primary School, Peterborough

Spooks

Tap, tap, tap. What could it be? *Tap, tip, tap, tap.* Where is it coming from? I'm too scared to open my eyes. *Tip, tap, tap.* Who could it be? I'm prepared to face terror. I open my eyes ... Phew! It's just the rain tapping away.

Magda Steele (10)
Longthorpe Primary School, Peterborough

Prometheus And The Vulture

Gods lived on Mount Olympus. The giant
Prometheus made people out of clay. Zeus puffed
life into them. Prometheus taught them everything
but Prometheus liked some fun, so he played a trick
on Zeus. Zeus punished Prometheus by tying him to
a rock where a vulture would eat his liver.

Emily Steele (10)
Longthorpe Primary School, Peterborough

The Mystery House

Creak! The door swung open. 'Wooo, whoo!'
'What was that?' I spun around, nothing was there.
It was coming closer. I could feel its warm breath
down my neck. I walked in. Everything was on the
floor, and even the windows were smashed!
'Boo!' Everything went black ... 'Argh!'

Richard Dodding (10)
Longthorpe Primary School, Peterborough

In My Garden

One day I was in my garden on my birthday. I heard a creepy noise ... someone opened the door and there was my birthday party and presents! 'Thank you Dad and Mum.' The end.

Daaim Ashraf (11)
Longthorpe Primary School, Peterborough

The Alien Tutor

It was coming closer. I fired my laser gun. It
wasn't working. Then it used its weapon homework.
'Leave now!' I shouted.
'Fine,' said my tutor. 'I'll see you next week.'
'Nooo!' I screamed.

Hussein-Abbas Ebrahim (9)
Longthorpe Primary School, Peterborough

Happy Birthday

I was looking through my window waiting for my present. Little did I know they went through the back door. I heard them whisper, '10, 9, 8, 7, 6, 5, 4, 3, 2, 1,' then they shouted, *'happy birthday!'*

Ben Johnson (10)
Longthorpe Primary School, Peterborough

The Night Before

The night before secondary school, 12.01. I was awake. Home alone. I went downstairs, the floorboards creaked. The wind howled, the trees brushed against the window. I heard a scream, a bang, then my bedroom window opened ... *Argh!*

Tayyaba Merali (10)
Longthorpe Primary School, Peterborough

Birthday

Mel woke up with a great start to the morning,
because it was her birthday. She went downstairs
with Mum and Dad and then grabbed her bag for
school and went. It was a strange day at school
because everyone was turning into aliens from
outer space.

Meghan Lawless (10)
Longthorpe Primary School, Peterborough

A Magic Spell That Goes Wrong

Sam was in his room, it was pitch-black. Sam went
for his tea, when Sam went back up the light was
on. A man was in there! Sam asked,
'What are you doing?'
He turned Sam into a monster then he disappeared.
Sam is a monster now!

Bethany Phillips (9)
Manea Community Primary School, March

An Alien Visiting Earth

He was up in bed, suddenly an enormous shooting
star came down. It was a star ship. The door
opened and an alien popped out.
'You're foolish human, you are destroying your
planet, goodbye!'
He went back to his planet where it was safe.

Ryan Davies (9)
Manea Community Primary School, March

An Alien Visiting Earth

Rob went down the stairs. He got the shock of his life. A green figure appeared in front of his eyes, he screamed! His mum rushed down the stairs, but it was too late, the alien had already gone. He told his mum but she didn't believe him.

Ryan Spry (9)
Manea Community Primary School, March

The Detective

The detective found the murderer's footsteps. He walked down the exhilarating dingy dark alley. He heard a bang and a croaky small voice saying, 'Help, help.' I saw the man with blood running down his face. *Drip-drop* it went. But he will return ...'

Jamie Francis (11)
Manea Community Primary School, March

The Age Of The Dinosaur

They were lost, no one was around. Suddenly a roar was heard. Four dinosaurs were fighting using their claws. They had fallen out. Eventually T-rex won. One dinosaur died, the other two dinosaurs were badly hurt. T-rex became the new leader and remained so until he died.

Daniel McDermott (9)
Manea Community Primary School, March

A Holiday Or Journey

He loaded them up for their holiday. At 4am they set up the awning. Suddenly it started to thunder, they were frightened, all the lights went off. They were all really scared. No one got to sleep all night.

Ashley Bullman (9)
Manea Community Primary School, March

A Magic Spell That Goes Wrong

A magic man tried a magic spell. The spell was so the man could juggle ten balls at a time. The spell went wrong. Then he could not even juggle with two balls. He was practising when the balls disappeared. He never juggled again.

Stevie Harrow (8)
Manea Community Primary School, March

Typical

The boy heard a sound, a shadow awoke. He got out of bed, there was a *tap, tap, tap.* The boy opened the door. There was an object in the shape of a dark, hairy alien in the cool breeze. He turned on the light. *Argh!*

Caitlin Wilby (9)
Manea Community Primary School, March

Unexplained Mystery

A shadow was creeping around the corner. A mystery, the shadow came closer, closer. Wait a minute, where's it gone? Quick let's go around the corner, see who's there. He'll catch him. He's not there. He'll have to turn into a detective.
'Andy, wake up,' Mum shouted.

Kelly Howell (9)
Manea Community Primary School, March

Manea Is The Capital

Many years ago between 1660 and 1686, King Charles the second decided that Manea should be the capital of England. In 1685, his head was cut off and he sadly died. Many years later, in the village of Manea, Charlemont Drive was built, in memory of Charles the second.

Sharon Howell (11)
Manea Community Primary School, March

The Haunted Beach Hut

One Saturday morning, the Scott's were looking for a beach hut to rent. The father of the Scott's found a perfect beach hut. It was a haunted hut and one by one the family disappeared. People say the ghost killed them or they fell through a never-ending earth hole.

George Burton (10)
Manea Community Primary School, March

The Flying Saucer

Rob was walking at 7pm, he saw lights in the air. He shone his torch into the night's sky.

'It's a spaceship,' Rob gasped.

The spaceship started to get lower and sucked Rob up in a beam of light. When they had Rob they blew up the city with lasers.

Nathan Dunstan (10)
Manea Community Primary School, March

The Magic Potion

Bongo is climbing a tree, finding a branch to sit on. He stumbles across a beaker and picks it up. It has a type of changing liquid in. Bongo starts to change flies into humans. The flies get hold of the potion and get closer and closer and *boom! He's* a fly!

Ashley Bridgement (10)
Manea Community Primary School, March

The Scientist's Scary House!

One day a boy was cycling through the woods when he found a scary house. This boy loved an adventure, so he went inside to take a look. He saw a scientist drop a corrosive acid on the floor. When it hit the ground there was no gravity forever.

Ryan Tibbles (11)
Manea Community Primary School, March

The Mystery Shadow

There was once a boy who was six years old. One dark, foggy night he woke up to find a shadow in the shape of a big scary fierce dog. The boy shouted for his parents. The shadow was getting closer and closer ...

Courtney Milner (11)
Manea Community Primary School, March

The Hidden Monster

Dr Burbs was quiet and sly, he was making a potion, made from acid, venom and gunpowder. After drinking the potion he turned into a monster who had a rifle for a hand. The monster shot and destroyed the laboratory.
After Burbs recovered he was never the same again.

Darcy Attrill (10)
Manea Community Primary School, March

The Magic Spell That Goes Wrong

Vicktore lived in the kingdom of Vicmum. Vicktore did a spell, when suddenly there was a puff of smoke that blew him down. He stood up and there she was. A witch who wanted to rule the world. Vicktore tried to catch her. She escaped and worked her evil magic.

Kate Baxter (9)
Manea Community Primary School, March

Terror Tower

It was a horrible, stormy night on the way to Terror Tower where Katie was staying. Terror Tower was no normal tower, it was haunted. Mary and Katie drank some orange juice that killed them, they were never seen again. Nobody knew how Terror Tower could hurt them.

Nikki Hopkin (10)
Manea Community Primary School, March

The Ghost

My friend and I saw something in my house window.
We went to check inside. Something felt strange
about my house. Then upstairs a door creaked ajar.
Suddenly we saw something white.
'A ghost!' I cried.
'Whooo,' it replied.
I recognised my other friend's voice, and laughed.

Charlie Levell   (10)
Notre Dame Preparatory School, Norwich

Vanishing Shoes

Once a little boy asked his mum if he could buy some new shoes. His mum said no. He got annoyed, so he got some money out of his mum's purse and walked out the door and went and bought some shoes. He put them on, and then he vanished.

Nyal Bayliss (10)
Notre Dame Preparatory School, Norwich

Best Friends

I started a new school. At first I didn't have any friends. I was miserable until Emma joined the same class two days after me. I went over to her at playtime and we talked. The teacher sat us together in class and we became best friends and still are.

Evie Mitchell (9)
Notre Dame Preparatory School, Norwich

A Lucky Walk In The Park

When my friend and I were walking in the park together, we heard a rustling in the leaves by the side of the swings ahead. We walked up to the noise. When we looked to see what it was, it was a cute dog huddled up. It was my dog!

Eleanor Lomax (10)
Notre Dame Preparatory School, Norwich

Happiness Appeared

Lucy was walking to school. Suddenly she heard a rumble, then a bark. She froze. She slowly turned around and stared at the bush, then moved forward, she was frightened. She sensed she saw yellow eyes, and a tail. She found her missing puppy. She was happy now.

Emily Greig (9)
Notre Dame Preparatory School, Norwich

The Monster Of Oz

There was a monster in a dark cave who did evil magic, he had more power than anyone. The wizard planned to kill the evil in the monster. The monster was invited to the Emerald City palace. Then the wizard killed the monster's evil heart. Now the monster is harmless.

Daniel Shakes (10)
Notre Dame Preparatory School, Norwich

Safari Nightmare

I was on Safari with my family when our truck flipped over! I awoke lying on leaves with a painful headache. I saw someone lying behind a tree. It was my sister, Laya! But where were Mum and Dad? We heard someone calling us, we froze, it was Mum!

Eleanor Murphy (10)
Notre Dame Preparatory School, Norwich

The Town Monster

There was a monster terrorising a town. One day a boy went out to kill it. He took a sword and a shield. When he got there he swung his sword five times and managed to slay the dragon. When he got back everybody had a big party.

Maddie Anderson (10)
Notre Dame Preparatory School, Norwich

The Fifty Pence Piece

The mouse trudged through the cold night. He had just found a beautifully crafted sword. Suddenly an evil street cat appeared. The mouse was frustrated with him, all he did was rob evil, weak, honest creatures. Taking the cat by surprise he struck out and killed it with the sword.

Kieran Ronaldson   (10)
Notre Dame Preparatory School, Norwich

The Cat

I opened my eyes, the sun was an unusual colour, as if it had had a red dye spilt on it. *Thud, thud,* went my heart, rapidly getting quicker as the monster got ever closer now. My heart was racing along like a train. *Miaow* went the monster. My cat.

Rory Woodhouse (11)
Notre Dame Preparatory School, Norwich

The Something

Something stirred in its sleep. As it crept forward, mouth drooling, it scented its prey. On the move, it came to the door. As the door creaked open and a shadow loomed and crept to the table taking up his small trident and lunged at his lovely delicious meal.

Jordan Wilson (11)
Notre Dame Preparatory School, Norwich

The Dream

My heart thumped against my ribcage. I was full of fear. I was alone in the heart of the ocean! I heard movement from behind a large rock. I spun round, still doggy-paddling. An enormous shark was coming at me! I screamed, my alarm clock rang and I woke up.

Sarah Tooby (11)
Notre Dame Preparatory School, Norwich

The Military Mission

The aircraft soared through the air over the besieged capital, firing at will. Avoiding the anti-aircraft guns, the aircraft jolted and was hit. 'Mayday, Mayday,' the pilot cried, falling, *boom!* The craft crashed, enemy men came to investigate the site, but there was no one left alive.

James Ticehurst (11)
Notre Dame Preparatory School, Norwich

The Creaking Noise!

Creak, creak, creak, it's coming! It's getting closer and closer. Oh no, I can smell its horrible breath. I can smell its stinky feet. I can feel it getting closer. Oh no, it's here.

'Rosemary, we have got to go to school now, hurry.' Phew, it's not the horrible monster.

Rosemary Hook (8)
Notre Dame Preparatory School, Norwich

The Woodcutters

The chainsaw sliced through the tree trunk like a knife through butter. After the tree trunk smashed to the ground cracking as it fell. The woodcutters cut it into pieces for the fire, not knowing how much habitat they had destroyed, like nests, burrows, killing birds and rabbits.

James Loftus (10)
Notre Dame Preparatory School, Norwich

The Corpse

The corpse lay sprawled on the marble floor. As he leant over it, a tear fell from a bloodshot eye, and as it hit the floor, it went up in a watery explosion, and echoed round the room. Wait, that wasn't a tear, that was a dying heartbeat, he's alive!

George Keeling (11)
Notre Dame Preparatory School, Norwich

The Robot

Furtively Colin crept down the deserted corridor,
his footsteps echoed metallically. His eyes darted
from side to side. There was a soft whirr. It was
here! He spun round. The corridor was empty. He
heard gunfire, bullets ripped into the ground
around him. He aimed, fired and hit.
'Subject terminated.'

George Kay (11)
Notre Dame Preparatory School, Norwich

The Thing

There I was, cornered, sweat was gushing down my neck. I heard a creak, the door was open. The landing light projected the thing's shadow. It was huge and hairy. It was baring its huge fangs. It pounced and I felt a wet tongue. It was only the dog.

Trystian James (11)
Notre Dame Preparatory School, Norwich

Playing In Goal

The terrible missile was soaring towards me with deadly accuracy. The pain would be terrible. As it flies through the air, all who resist fall. It must hit me. But no it has missed. One thousand eyes are on me. Oh how I hate playing in goal!

Stephen Harsley   (11)
Notre Dame Preparatory School, Norwich

Captured

John yelled out in pain as he was thrown into the dark, dirty cell. There was no way out apart from overriding a twelve digit code, then getting past two armed security guards and next he would have to find a space pod that would take him to Earth.

Philip Fulcher (11)
Notre Dame Preparatory School, Norwich

The Scary Evening

One lovely evening there standing at the window was a black shadow. Then there was a knock on the door, what was it? Was it a ghost or could it be a horse? She opened the door to meet her long-lost mother named Megan.

Sasha Broad (10)
Notre Dame Preparatory School, Norwich

A Deep Mystery

I went in a dark room and then a hand reached out
to get me.
'Come with me,' said a voice.
I followed it up the stairs and up some more until
we got to the very top. It opened a door.
'Wake up, or you'll be late!' said Dad.

Mamiroro Emore (8)
Notre Dame Preparatory School, Norwich

Oh Drat

One day there were three girls, Cleme, Savanna and Vilma. Savanna had a knife and stabbed Vilma and there was lots of blood all over the floor. Cleme saw blood running down Savanna's arm and Vilma was dead. Savanna and Cleme were cheering but Vilma was still alive.
'Oh drat!'

Savanna Guthrie (11)
St Michael's CE VA Primary School, St Albans

The Egg With A Daisy

On a wall, an old egg with a daisy, sat in the breeze.
She was purple, with a pink silk dress. For hair, she
had daisies. Every day, Eggy would hop down off
the wall at noon to go shopping. One day, as she was
jumping, she slipped. Oh no!

Wynona Dekker (10)
St Michael's CE VA Primary School, St Albans

Cindy's Wish

Cindy was unhappy. She saw a notice,
Disco on Friday.
Cindy told her stepmother, who wouldn't let her go.
On Friday her sisters went. Her mother was
standing in front ...
'What do you want?'
'I want to go.'
She was allowed to go. The prince asked her to
dance!

Vilma Kallio (10)
St Michael's CE VA Primary School, St Albans

Devils In The Night

George went out and bought all the toys in Waitrose. He lugged the bag home. When he got home he saw the toys all had a rip in them, so he threw them in the bin. But the toys started climbing up the ivy. He remembered the window was open!

Jake Branagan (9)
St Michael's CE VA Primary School, St Albans

The Night Scare

As I tiptoed down the stairs, I tripped and fell into deep space. Everything was dark. Then pairs of glowing eyes lit up at me! All of a sudden they disappeared and then I saw a shaft of light. I woke up, it was morning.

Eleanor Morton-Smith (9)
St Michael's CE VA Primary School, St Albans

Vampire's Teeth

George lay awake hiding under the cover. Suddenly a giant shadow appeared in the shape of a vampire, he nearly fainted at the sight of the shadow. It walked in and bit him ... but the vampire couldn't get his teeth out. He yanked. Soon they came out of his mouth.

Ryan Cobb (9)
St Michael's CE VA Primary School, St Albans

The Ant

The ant lay there, blood trickling from its body. Suddenly *thud, thud, thud*, what was it? It was the man-eating spider! Then there was a cry of pain. 'Argh!' But it wasn't from the ant, the ant had victory over the spider … but how?

Emma Pinney (9)
St Michael's CE VA Primary School, St Albans

Midnight Fright

Slipping down the stairs missing out the creaky ones, she made it to the kitchen ... alone ... in the dark. She aimed for the stove, she wanted a midnight snack.

'Pancakes I think,' she whispered. She gently turned on the stove. When flames arose from it, Sarah disappeared without a trace.

Sarah Fabian (9)
St Michael's CE VA Primary School, St Albans

A Dark Seaside

It was dark at the seaside. The waves rolling in on the sand. Leaving behind a white froth on the beach. I looked up, a darker figure was appearing on the horizon. It was coming closer to me. It was another girl, my age, but she looked a little strange

...

Emma Ferreira (9)
St Michael's CE VA Primary School, St Albans

The Thing

I was sitting by the lake watching the blood-red creature. Its emerald eyes gleaming back in the icy cold water. The creature sank back into the water. I walked back to my house. Never to return ...

Carys Hogan (10)
St Michael's CE VA Primary School, St Albans

His Last Words

He lay unconscious having been hit by a shield. He woke. Nobody was there. The battle was over. His hair was mingled with blood and bits of shield. He ran to the great hall, nobody was there ...
'How come ... ? What the ... ?' were his last croaky words ...

Joseph Zacaroli (9)
St Michael's CE VA Primary School, St Albans

State Moscow

Alex was sitting in a trench. He knew State Moscow were after him.

Suddenly he heard the sound of spades getting louder and louder ... Then he saw them and vanished into thin air.

Alex was falling, he felt himself hit the ground. He was in State Moscow Base.

William Pettitt (9)
St Michael's CE VA Primary School, St Albans

Things That Go Click In The Night

Click ... what was that? It came from the door ... I went to the door. It was so quiet. I could hear the tap dripping. I neared the door ... at first, I thought someone was following me ... I turned the knob. Locked ... There was nowhere to go ... it was hopeless ...

Luca Hames (10)
St Michael's CE VA Primary School, St Albans

The Noise On The Roof

I was lying in bed and suddenly heard a noise on the roof. A noise like ssss flap. I clambered out of bed, went downstairs. I got the ladder, I went up to the roof and before me was a huge, flying snake.
'Wake up now,' said Mum.

Isobel Ryan-Dalton (9)
St Michael's CE VA Primary School, St Albans

The Boy With A Toy

Thomas loved Teddy. While he was playing, Teddy got lost! After a while Thomas noticed that Teddy was lost. He told his mum.

His mum said, 'Go and look in the garden.'

So Thomas looked in the garden, but Teddy was nowhere to be seen. So he cried.

Prasasdini Fernando (10)

St Michael's CE VA Primary School, St Albans

Lottie In Flight

I walked through the park. I found a clearing. It looked strangely like a desert island. What's that? I heard a noise. A rustling noise. I curiously walked into the clearing. There it was a pteradactyl. Suddenly something lifted me on its back.

Emma Dovey (9)
St Michael's CE VA Primary School, St Albans

Wet War

The sniper sat in silence with his gun. He knew the enemy tank would come. He loaded and aimed at the turn in the road. He was wet, cold ... It had been raining and the mud was everywhere. Then, suddenly, he heard a low rumble, then round the corner came ...

Jack Crawford (9)
St Michael's CE VA Primary School, St Albans

The Dog's Unhappy Ending

Once there was a dog called Lucy, she was fast asleep. Suddenly the door slammed shut and she was going very fast around. She was getting very wet and she was spinning faster and faster. The dog was drowning ... Then Karen opened the door. It was over.

Ellyn Deacon (9)
St Michael's CE VA Primary School, St Albans

Big Spider

I was in the bedroom. The door was locked. On my bed was a spider. I was so scared, I screamed. The spider scuttled around. I screamed again louder this time, and it came nearer to me. I picked it up frightened, and it tickled. I was not scared anymore.

Marika Buck (9)
St Michael's CE VA Primary School, St Albans

The Unexpected

I didn't expect it to happen as I lay in my bed. Who does expect to be snatched out of their bed into the darkness of the London Underground? Shoved into a corner with only the light of the trains to keep me company, as gas started filling my lungs.

Anna Murgatroyd (11)
St Michael's CE VA Primary School, St Albans

The Forgotten Man

He awoke with a start ... Who was he ... ? Where was he ... ? All sense of time and place had left him. He dug deep into his memory ... He found nothing. What limitless tide of evil had swept him away? He knew nothing, he felt nothing, he was nothing.

Gabriel Mead (11)
St Michael's CE VA Primary School, St Albans

The Tree That Walked

Chop, the loggers in the rainforest were in a logging spot. The tree moved behind them ...
'Do you hear something?'
They were trampled seconds later. An angry scream was heard. Around an hour later 380 walking trees were in a clearing. They had sighted the loggers' town.

James Cole (11)
St Michael's CE VA Primary School, St Albans

Untitled

It walked onwards, towards the orphanage. It was small and squishy, like a hedgehog. Though it had no spikes ... but wait ... it was growing arms and they were sprouting hands. It was getting taller and more human, it was ... 'Mum, who are you?'

Sophie Pinney (11)
St Michael's CE VA Primary School, St Albans

Captured By A Dragon

John crept up to the pile of treasure trying not to make a noise.
Suddenly the dragon was alerted to John's presence. He snatched John, pondering how to eat him. 'I'll sleep on it,' he decided.
John was tied up, but found a knife, he was free! Or was he … ?

Declan Baldwin (11)
St Michael's CE VA Primary School, St Albans

The Mission

Standing frozen, not making a sound, he mustn't
spot me. With my rifle loaded up, ready to shoot.
He has seen me, what shall I do? Run. But no, I
can't, then I must fight.

Gaby Medforth (11)
St Michael's CE VA Primary School, St Albans

The Wizard

He shot the harpoon at the great white shark.
Bang! He hit.
'Ow! That hurt!' Instead of a great white he had hit
a man in white robes. He looked like a wizard – he
was. He healed where the harpoon had struck.
'That's better,' he said. 'You will pay!'

Charles Deacon (11)
St Michael's CE VA Primary School, St Albans

The Tortoise

How old is it? Where did it come from? I sat
staring at its beauty. What had it seen in its past ...
? So delicate and so wise. Everyone of them so
slow. Has it come from another race, an
undiscovered race?

Jack Kempton (10)
St Michael's CE VA Primary School, St Albans

Bull Fight Bonanza

Shimmering muscle, silk black shoulder to tail
charging full-pelt at me. Intimidated by the beast,
I froze as still as a stone. Petrified. Suddenly a
jolt of energy took me and I leapt in the air. It
collided fully with the boundary, I gathered my
spear and stabbed it.

Andrew Sears-Black (10)
St Michael's CE VA Primary School, St Albans

Hallway Nightmares

The man enters a hallway lined with windows. The windows blow open. A bone-chilling wind swirls round. Water dripping echoes round the hall. The man freezes. Ice-cold blood trickles down his back. A hairy, bloodstained, talloned hand rests on the man's shoulder. He turns pearly white, argh!

Cameron Roy (10)
St Michael's CE VA Primary School, St Albans

Invasion!

Earth was at war. The shripnels led by the Shripnoid were invading Earth. General Slavenik leading the humans fought bravely with his remaining troops. But Earth was lost and he and his army were forced onto the moon. There, General Slavenik had plans for a great charge to save Earth.

Alistair Roy (10)
St Michael's CE VA Primary School, St Albans

The Spider Bite

Ow … something bit me. I felt the blood pulsating out of my leg. I saw my family hovering above me crying. I leant in to hug them, I drifted right through them. I was evolving into a creature of the night. I was Ghost Spider, the creature of death.

Cleme Lewis (10)
St Michael's CE VA Primary School, St Albans

Escape

Jim was ten, he lived in London, 1940. Fire was breathing like a dragon in London. Oh no, it was the air raid. Jim ran, ran as fast as his legs could carry him. Doors are locked, what can he do?

Nicholas Sutton (10)
St Michael's CE VA Primary School, St Albans

Dragon

Charlotte went on holiday. She went to a rocky beach. She saw a cave. Charlotte heard a noise, it was a dragon. It went to eat her but she screamed *'No!'* and ordered it to be her friend and they were best friends forever and ever and lived happily forever.

Charlotte Cooper (10)
Summerfield Combined School, Milton Keynes

Dragon Alert

A dragon came to the city for food so the people had to give him animals. When they ran out of animals, the only choice was to vote out people. The scientist was picked, locked outside. He called for help. An alien arrived, killed the dangerous dragon. City was saved.

Sam Hughes (10)
Summerfield Combined School, Milton Keynes

Untitled

Little Red was in the woods. A big bad dragon popped out and put her to sleep. He took her to his submarine and tied her up. When she woke he said, 'You're the powerful one, fire up your powers.'
'No!'
Suddenly Granny appeared and shot the devilish dragon!

James Whitaker (9)
Summerfield Combined School, Milton Keynes

Monster Mystery

We were sprinting through the woods and suddenly
Viper was there. I could hear him running after me
and Jimmy. But I tripped and fell over a branch and
he was catching up, while I'm still on the floor.
Jimmy came to the rescue and whacked Viper on
the head.

Sophie Sankey (10)
Summerfield Combined School, Milton Keynes

The Ancient Leaf Of Time

There was a young dinosaur who ate a leaf. That leaf was magic, he then blew up and found himself in the 21st century. He then bred lots of dinos with a golden eagle and all the dinogles ate the human race. Suddenly Haley's Comet hit the Earth ...

Kristijan Carlsson (10)
Summerfield Combined School, Milton Keynes

The Mask Of Horror

There's a big ugly mask in a cave where children play. There were hundreds of people that didn't believe in the mask and went up there and were turned to stone. A great warrior of strength and wit went to destroy the mask. No one saw him again.

Anila Abbas (10)
Summerfield Combined School, Milton Keynes

Heracles Death

Once upon a time there was a young man called
Heracles. One day Heracles was summoned to
death. Heracles had to kill a griffin. Heracles drew
his sword but it was made of wood. The griffin ran
over to Heracles and with one big bite, Heracles
came to death.

Ryan Watson (10)
Summerfield Combined School, Milton Keynes

Red Riding Hood Gone Wrong

One day Mother told me to go and visit Granny, so I did. In the forest I met Wolfy and we became mates. We killed Granny and lived in her house, spending all the cash that she'd won in a game of poker. Ha, ha, ha! It was great!

Damask Talary-Brown (9)
Summerfield Combined School, Milton Keynes

Little Blue Riding Hood

There was a girl called Little Blue Riding Hood. She went to see her Granny. The wolf found out where she was and gobbled her up, plus the woodcutter came along with an axe, striking the wolf, but it bounced off back into the man's neck, the wolf wins!

April Scott (10)
Summerfield Combined School, Milton Keynes

Stuart And The Bermuda Triangle

A man called Stuart was piloting his plane through the Bermuda Triangle. Suddenly it stopped. It was captured by dragons. They were holding onto the plane. Stuart shot bullets at them but they shot them straight back at the plane. It crashed and Stuart turned into a dragon too.

Bilaal Ali (10)
Summerfield Combined School, Milton Keynes

The Dragon With Three Heads

In a kingdom far away lived King Arthur and Princess Fiona. They were scared of a three-headed dragon. Ross the dragon slayer came. Ross had a magical white dragon, but the bad dragon killed the good dragon. So Ross stabbed the dragon in the heart!

Scott Parker (10)
Summerfield Combined School, Milton Keynes

The Green Man

One day a man called Tim got kidnapped by a green man. Tim was sent down a drain. Down the drain there were lots of green men singing a bizarre song in a different language. The song put Tim to sleep. When he woke he was a green man.

Kyle Andrews (10)
Summerfield Combined School, Milton Keynes

Apparitions

Derelict floorboards, cracked walls submerged in darkness. An abrasive cacophony of disturbing moans engulfed Jack, as he ran fervently wishing it would end! To be in the least conspicuous was to sign a death sentence! Suddenly, a ghostly hand erupted from a wall crevice!

Alex Howes (12)
West Earlham Middle School, Norwich

The Dark Forest

Anna was wandering along the narrow path in the woods, where the trees were whistling. A branch snapped ... *Creak,* branches swayed in the breeze. Anna felt scared, she didn't know what was happening. *Snap!* What was that?
Out from the shadows stepped Anna's mum!
'Where were you?' said Anna's mum.

Hayley Clarke (10)
Wimbotsham & Stow Community School, Kings Lynn

A Magic Spell That Goes Wrong

Add one worm, half a spoonful of blood, three ostrich eggs, six spoonfuls of rabbit-droppings. One teaspoon of dust and two spoonfuls of frog fat. Boil for six minutes, then add one drop of vinegar and then ... *bang!*

Alice Harness   (10)

Wimbotsham & Stow Community School, Kings Lynn

Rustling!

Elle looked behind her but nothing was there. *Creak, creak!* She looked around again, but nothing was there, her palms sweating, her hair stood on head. The bush was rustling, she stood back in fright as a creature emerged from the bush ... it was ... a squirrel running away scared!

Ellen Atkinson (10)
Wimbotsham & Stow Community School, Kings Lynn

What's In The Woods?

Walking alone. Woods of trees appearing. Moonlight brightens the sky. Looking around I hear rustling, I stop suddenly. I feel a hand touch my back. Strikes of lightning appear in the bright sky. A voice whispers into my ear. A ghost appears. I am rooted to the ground.

Danielle Lamont (11)
Wimbotsham & Stow Community School, Kings Lynn

The Sleeping Creature!

It lays there unmoving. Carefully, I move towards
it, making sure I don't wake it. It's growing bigger
and bigger until it erupts! *Ping!*
'Mum, the cakes are ready.'

Corinne Jenkinson (10)
Wimbotsham & Stow Community School, Kings Lynn

The Hole

Joan ran frantically towards the school gate. When she arrived where the gates had been there was a big black hole! She stepped closer, then again. All of a sudden three more appeared. They all moved closer to her!

'Wake up, rise and shine you're going to be late for school.'

Barrie Fletcher (11)
Wimbotsham & Stow Community School, Kings Lynn

Shrek 1

Princess Fiona has been locked in a castle by her parents. Prince Charming tries to rescue her before anyone else does, but Shrek and Donkey get there and they aim to save her from the castle. Donkey attracts the dragon so Shrek can get into the castle and rescue her.

Lauren Cox (10)
Wimbotsham & Stow Community School, Kings Lynn

The Cake

Constantly she stirred the cauldron with her wand.
Abigail, the witch, was putting powder in; she
added frogs' legs, frogs' guts and then acid. She
put the potion in the oven and turned it on. Abigail
waited and waited, sitting at the table, until ... the
cake was ready to eat.

Abbie Silsbury (11)
Wimbotsham & Stow Community School, Kings Lynn

The Sound Of Laughter

As I ran through the forest I could hear people laughing ... laughing at me. I kept on running as fast as I could. But then, I stopped so suddenly that I fell forward into mud. My face felt like it was being hit by a pillow.
'Wake up Amy.'

Emma Bates (11)
Wimbotsham & Stow Community School, Kings Lynn

The Seeker

He was there, I knew he was. He had come back, back into hiding. Ready to pounce. He came when the countdown began. Ready to strike, ready to make his getaway. Then he ran, I followed, I caught. I was the winner. It was his turn to count.

Samuel Warner (11)
Wimbotsham & Stow Community School, Kings Lynn

Dinosaurs

I could see it. Chasing me through the jungle. I was cut off, it had me. Then it happened … a storm. The monster was distracted and ran away. It came back for me. It found me! It caught me, it ate me! *Beep! Beep!* My alarm clock went off.

Jack Hunt   (10)
Wimbotsham & Stow Community School, Kings Lynn

Will He Be Found?

Mell sneaked up the stairs into her bedroom. She heard a creak ... two more, where could he be? Mell was searching and searching. She crept quietly back into the bathroom. She heard breathing, deep, heavy breathing.
'*Boo!* Found you. Your turn to hide now,' said James.

Myfanwy-Kate Squires (11)
Wimbotsham & Stow Community School, Kings Lynn

Jog In The Woods

Tom was on his weekly jog. He saw a flash of light. Suddenly it got closer and closer. Tom ran as fast as he could. The flash followed faster and faster. Tom didn't stop, he ran. With a flash and a roar the Landrover sped past Tom.

Jedd Desborough (10)
Wimbotsham & Stow Community School, Kings Lynn

Hide-And-Seek

Roger was looking for George in the cellar. He looked everywhere and couldn't find him, then he found a door with a key on the other side. He couldn't get it open. He got a hammer and smashed the hinges off and found a dead body on the other side.

Ashley Kidd (11)
Wimbotsham & Stow Community School, Kings Lynn

The Sighting

'Look! What's that? I cannot see it's too misty.'
'Most probably a boat.'
'In this weather?'
'Might be the Loch Ness monster.'
'Nar it doesn't exist.'
'Really, what's that then?'
'I don't know.'
'Shouldn't we go see what it is?'
'OK.'
Suddenly it all became clear – it was a boat.

Brad Wiles (11)
Wimbotsham & Stow Community School, Kings Lynn

The Dark Street

Kirsty was walking down the dark street when suddenly she heard a sound. It stopped and then went again, this sound was scaring her. She stopped and listened. It went again and again and when she got to the end of the street, she heard a big *bang!*

Billie McKenzie (10)

Wimbotsham & Stow Community School, Kings Lynn

Peter Pan

Peter Pan and the Lost Boys were trying to save Wendy, but Captain Hook had Wendy. Peter Pan and the Lost Boys had to make a plan. Peter Pan had an idea, it was to wipe out Captain Hook. Peter Pan's idea worked. Peter Pan got Wendy back finally.

Jon Corley (11)
Wimbotsham & Stow Community School, Kings Lynn

Information

We hope you have enjoyed reading this book - and that you will continue to enjoy it in the coming years.

If you like reading and writing, drop us a line or give us a call and we'll send you a free information pack. Alternatively visit our website at **www.youngwriters.co.uk**

Write to:

**Young Writers Information,
Remus House,
Coltsfoot Drive,
Peterborough,
PE2 9JX**

Tel: (01733) 890066